THE LAND OF MILK AND HONEY

THE LAND OF MILK AND HONEY

An Introduction to the Geography of Israel

JOHN A. BECK

CONCORDIA PUBLISHING HOUSE · SAINT LOUIS

To John and Lorraine Beck, who ignited in me both
a love for the Lord and a passion for travel.

Thanks . . . Jack

Published by Concordia Publishing House
3558 S. Jefferson Ave., St. Louis, MO 63118-3968
1-800-325-3040 • www.cph.org

Copyright © 2006 John A. Beck

Manufactured in the United States of America

Library of Congress Cataloging in Publication Data
Beck, John A., 1956–
    The land of milk and honey : an introduction to the geography of Israel / John A. Beck.
        p. cm.
    Includes bibliographical references and index.
    ISBN 0-7586-0056-9
    1. Bible--Geography. 2. Palestine--Historical geography. I. Title.
    BS630.B37 2006
    220.9'1—dc22
                                                        2005038045

1 2 3 4 5 6 7 8 9 10   15 14 13 12 11 10 09 08 07 06

CONTENTS

Regions of Biblical Israel

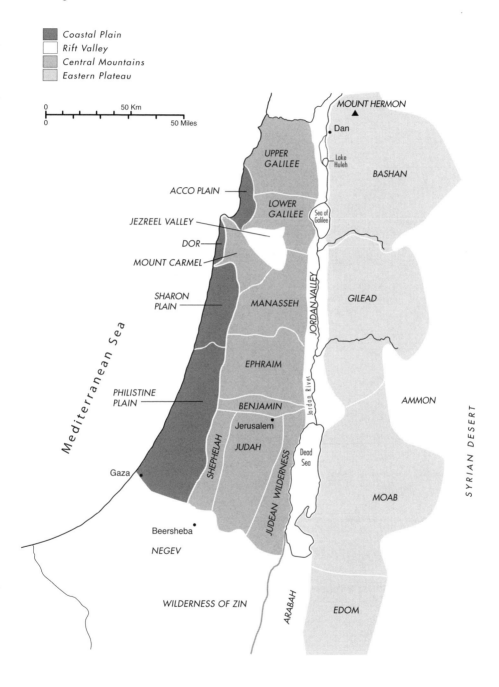

Legend:
- Coastal Plain
- Rift Valley
- Central Mountains
- Eastern Plateau

0   50 Km
0   50 Miles

MOUNT HERMON ▲

Dan

UPPER GALILEE

Lake Huleh

BASHAN

ACCO PLAIN

LOWER GALILEE

JEZREEL VALLEY

Sea of Galilee

DOR

MOUNT CARMEL

Mediterranean Sea

SHARON PLAIN

MANASSEH

GILEAD

JORDAN VALLEY

EPHRAIM

Jordan River

PHILISTINE PLAIN

BENJAMIN

AMMON

Jerusalem

SHEPHELAH

JUDAH

Dead Sea

Gaza

JUDEAN WILDERNESS

SYRIAN DESERT

MOAB

Beersheba

NEGEV

WILDERNESS OF ZIN

ARABAH

EDOM

Cities and features of Israel

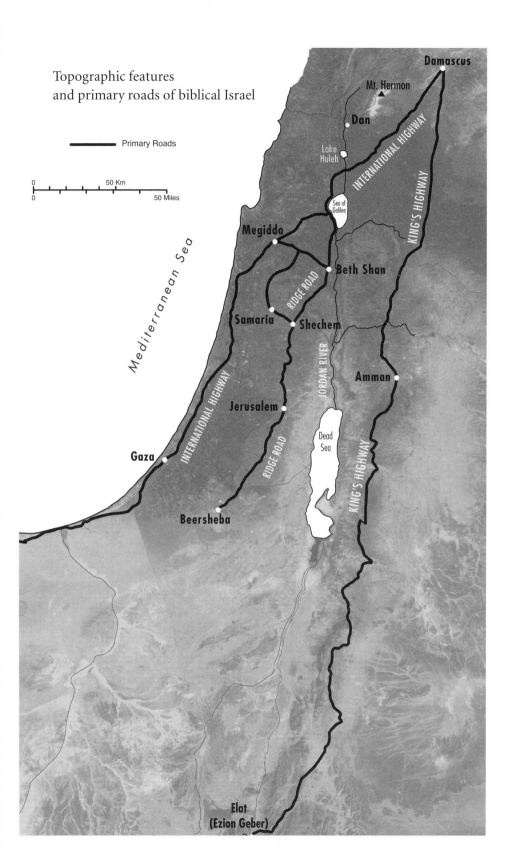

Topographic features
and primary roads of biblical Israel

—— Primary Roads

0   50 Km
0   50 Miles

Damascus

Mt. Hermon

Dan

Lake
Huleh

Sea of
Galilee

Megiddo

Beth Shan

INTERNATIONAL HIGHWAY

KING'S HIGHWAY

RIDGE ROAD

Samaria

Shechem

JORDAN RIVER

Amman

Mediterranean Sea

INTERNATIONAL HIGHWAY

Jerusalem

Dead
Sea

Gaza

RIDGE ROAD

KING'S HIGHWAY

Beersheba

Elat
(Ezion Geber)

INTRODUCTION

We give unique and special names to unique and special places. No one standing on the rim of the Grand Canyon at sunrise will disagree that the name "grand" fits the view of the canyon before them. Likewise, no one who experiences the geography of the Promised Land will disagree with the appropriateness of God's name for this special place. He called it the land of milk and honey. This name not only distinguishes the Promised Land and its natural resources from the desolate deserts around it but also alludes to the geographical diversity found here. In the north, generous precipitation favors the farmer. Rain gives rise to rich agricultural fields that flower and bloom, providing natural resources the bees need to make *honey*. In the south, dryer conditions favor pastoral pursuits. Here the Bedouin children tend the family goat herd that is the source of the *milk* they drink. When God speaks of this entire land, He labels it "a land flowing with milk and honey" (Deuteronomy 11:9), acknowledging the dominance of agriculture in the north and pastoral pursuits in the south.

As proper as that name is, the Promised Land is more than just a land of milk and honey. It is also a land of hope. No place in the world could dare claim such a title after the fall of Adam and Eve into sin. God's creation had become a hopeless place with painful childbirth, weeds in gardens, and death. God's wonderful world had become a hopeless place, and no human being had the power to change it. What no mortal could do, God did. He restored hope to a ruined world. And He did it in this special place. After God announced that Abram's family members would be more numerous than the dust of the earth, He told Abram to look in every direction and take in the expanse of land that his family would own (Genesis 13:16–17). On that very land from that very family, the promised Savior would be born. As our substitute, this Redeemer would do what no human could do, and He would undo what every human had done. Jesus would live the perfect life each of us owed to God but could not pay. He would suffer the punishment for our sins so we would never again have to fear that God's anger would be exhausted on us. As this rescue mission would be staged here, the land that is geographically the land of milk and honey becomes, theologically, the land of hope.

Stories throughout the Bible are linked to this land and this hope. Here Joshua conquers Jericho, Deborah encourages Barak on Mount Tabor, Samuel leads a reformation in Benjamin, and Solomon builds the temple in Jerusalem. Each of these acts, and countless others, play a role in God's rescue plan. In the New Testament, anticipation gives way to reality as this land becomes the stage for Jesus' earthly ministry. He is born in the village of Bethlehem. He preaches and heals in the synagogue at Capernaum. He calms the water on the Sea of Galilee. In Jerusalem, Jesus dies on a cross and rises from the dead, proving Himself to be our Savior.

The unfolding of all these events in just this place is no historical accident. God selected and designed this land to be the stage for this divine drama. Barry Beitzel asserts, "God prepared the Promised Land for His chosen people with the same degree of care that He prepared His chosen people for the Promised Land."[1] This reality creates a challenge for us as Bible readers. To appreciate the selection of this land we must become both geographer and theologian. Only then will we see that this is both the land of milk and honey and the land of hope. The book you hold in your hands intends to honor that thesis. It will introduce you to the geography of this land with an unmistakable awareness of its theological role in bringing salvation to the world.

Perhaps you have come to think of geography only in connection with maps. While it is true that the biblical geographer has more than a passing interest in maps, they are only tools that help us visualize the various dimensions of the land carefully shaped by the Creator's hand. Geography pursues the surface contours and features. It inquires about the geological composition of the mountains, valleys, and hills. It studies the plant life and animal communities that live on its surface. It examines the climate and the water resources offered by the land. It inquires about where people built their homes, how they traveled, and how they employed the land to sustain their lives. Geography also charts the drawing and redrawing of political borders and boundaries.

These elements of the land that geographers pursue with such passion play a critical role in our biblical reading because they make a significant contribution to the history and culture of those who live in the land. Geography establishes boundaries and creates opportunities. It conditions and directs everyday tasks. The truth of this thesis may be observed in your own life. The type of coats you keep in your closet, the kind of food you will eat at your next meal, and how you travel are all significantly influenced by your geographical setting. The same is equally true for the men and women we meet in the Bible. They, like we, lived their lives under the influence of time and place. Where they met to fight their battles, where they built their cities, how they obtained their water, and when they planted their field crops all depended on the unique geography of Israel. Consequently, the more we understand about the place where they lived, the better we will understand their story. When completing his translation of the Old Testament into Latin, Jerome moved to Bethlehem in order to steep himself more deeply in the geography and culture of this land. His experience in the Promised Land led him to write these words: "Just as those who have seen Athens understand Greek history better, and just as those who have seen Troy understand the words of the poet Virgil, thus one will comprehend the Holy Scriptures with a clearer understanding who has seen the land of Judah with his own eyes. . . . "[2] The same observation is expressed by geographer Yohanan Aharoni: "In the land of the Bible, geography and history are so deeply interwoven that neither can be really understood without the help of the other. Without an awareness of the stage, the action of the drama cannot be fully understood."[3]

So the study of physical geography leads to an investigation of historical geography and culture that enhances our Bible reading. Physical geography also leads to an investigation of the artful use of geography in the writing process. We call this literary phenomenon "literary geography." As the inspired authors of the Bible wrote, they were led by the Holy Spirit to include geography in the telling of their stories and in the shaping of their poetry. It is clear that they intended to shape their readers through the careful use of geographical references. Perhaps you have been in the habit of reading quickly past references to place names, topography, geology, or natural resources. Literary geography challenges us to slow our reading pace and ask how the biblical author may be employing geography to inform our understanding of God's truth and solicit our trust in Him.

This is not to say that all biblical authors employ geography to the same degree. Some pages of the Bible are devoid of geographical references while others are filled with them. Consider the virtual tour of Israel's geography that the reader receives in Psalm 104. In verse after verse, we see references to rain, wind, mountains, valleys, springs, wild animals, plants, trees, the sea, and seasons. It goes without saying that the better we understand the geography of Israel, the more we will understand the message of this psalm.

At other times, geographical references can be more subtle. In Matthew 4:13, the geographical reference signaling a change in Jesus' place of residence can easily be lost among the other details of the chapter. The author reports, "Leaving Nazareth, He went and lived in Capernaum." But this change of residence is filled with much greater significance than is first apparent. Jesus moves from a small and remote Jewish village to an international city that sits astride the International Highway. Thus Jesus establishes His base of operations at a spot where His words and actions will be carried far and wide along with the commodities traveling to Egypt and Persia. "Leaving Nazareth, He went and lived in Capernaum." The words may be few and unassuming, but their message is powerful.

There is clearly much to learn from the geographical references made in our Bible. But the moment we attend to these geographical references, we need to guard against another danger. This danger is the risk of reading our own local, geographical experience into the terms used by the ancient authors. Let us consider rain for a moment. When the biblical writers employ the word *rain*, we immediately place that idea within the realm of our own cultural context. For many reading this book, rain will have a more negative connotation. Rain spoils picnics and ruins vacations. Although we all know the nurturing affect of rainfall, the local weather reporter offers the news of coming rain apologetically, and with the encouragement that things will "improve" soon. By contrast, rain is not considered as something bad in Israel, but as something good and even precious. "Improvement" in the weather in Israel means that it will rain. Precipitation is so scarce and infrequent in this region, that its arrival brings celebration. When the writer of Proverbs 16:15 wants to describe the favorable demeanor of a king, he uses the rain cloud as a positive metaphor. "When a king's face brightens, it means life; his favor is like a rain cloud in spring." Thus it is critical not only to notice geographical terms used by biblical authors but also to check our understanding of those terms by linking them to their Middle Eastern context.

When Bible readers pay close attention to geographical references and view them through the eyes of a Middle Eastern resident, they will gain fresh insights into familiar stories and find answers to difficult questions associated with those stories. For example, how is it that experienced fishermen are caught on the Sea of Galilee during a fierce windstorm (Matthew 8:23–27)? When we study the geography of Israel, we learn that more than one type of wind might impact the lake basin. While some of those winds are very predictable, others will strike the Sea of Galilee without any warning. In the coming pages, you will learn about the sharquia winds. Given the right atmospheric conditions, these fierce and unpredictable winds dive from the mountain heights above the Sea of Galilee, creating exactly the conditions for boaters described by the Gospel writer. It is undoubtedly this kind of wind that caught these experienced fishermen by surprise.

If you love to study God's Word and are passionate about finding insights into texts like these, you have come to the right place. This book offers you an introduction to the geography of Israel, the land of milk, honey, and hope. Here you will come to appreciate the critical location of this land and the dearth of natural resources that makes this place a land that fosters faith. Region by region, you will come to know the geo-political divisions and centers, the topography, geology, hydrology, climate, urbanization, land use, and transportation that impacts the history, culture, and literature of the Bible. Christians who make a trip to Israel often say that they will never read their Bibles the same way again. That is my hope for you as you take this virtual tour through Israel. After reading this book, you will develop a greater sensitivity to the use of geography in the Bible. Its historical events and the actions of ordinary citizens will become more meaningful as you view them in their own time and place. In the end, my greatest hope is that you will obtain a clearer impression of God's message to you in those passages where He has elected to use geography to shape that message.

THE LAND OF ISRAEL

In the pages that follow, we will take a walk through the Promised Land and see it just as Abraham or John would have seen it. We will explore one area at a time, pausing to observe all that we see around us. Region by region, we will examine the wonders of God's creation in the landforms, the weather, and the water sources. We will observe the day-to-day activities of people responding to that geography as they tend their agricultural fields, press their olives, and conduct commerce. But before we step in for a closer look at this land, we will step back and view it as a whole while asking questions related to the entire Promised Land. What names were given to this land throughout its history? How large is this land? How does the land's geography vary between the sea and the desert? With what kinds of plant and animal communities did people in the Bible interact? Why did the Lord select this land to be the Promised Land?

NAMES OF THE LAND

We have already seen that the Lord Himself described Israel as the land of milk and honey. Throughout history, humans have also named the land and in the paragraphs that follow, we will survey some of those names. We will limit ourselves to a discussion of those that are of greatest significance to biblical history.

The Egyptians called this land "Canaan." During the second millennium BC, they used this name to designate the southern extent of their holdings in Asia.[1] Before the discovery of the Nuzi archives (fifteenth century BC), it was assumed that the term *Canaan* was linked to the idea of "lowland." This view was supported by texts like Numbers 13:29 and Joshua 5:1 that suggest the Canaanites lived in the lower elevations of the country. But with the discovery of the Nuzi archives, another intriguing etymology of the word *Canaan* came to the foreground. The Nuzi word *kinahhu* refers to a red-purple dye that is derived from the murex seashell found along the Mediterranean coastline. This highly prized dye was harvested by those living along the coast to produce expensive purple garments. You may recall that while Paul was traveling in Macedonia, he met a believer by the name of Lydia who sold this expensive, purple cloth (Acts 16:14). It is possible that the name of the Canaanites and the name of the land they occupied is linked to this dye industry because they lived along the Mediterranean Coast.[2]

This land is also called Palestine or Judah. The history of that naming is a bit more complex. The Promised Land was called Palestine as early as the eighth century BC by the Assyrian Adadnirari III (810–783 BC) who employed it to designate the coastal regions occupied by the Philistines. In the fifth century BC, the Greek historian Herodotus referred to the entire Mediterranean coastlands as Palestine.[3] At nearly the same time, Jewish writers used the name Judah for their land. At first, this name was applied only to the southern part of the Promised Land held by the Israelites after the Babylonian Exile. However, in the years that followed, the Hasmonean kings who expanded Jewish holdings into the northern portions of the Promised Land called all the land they ruled Judah. When the Romans conquered the country, they adopted the name Judah for the same area. However, following the Bar-Kokhba revolt against Rome in the second century AD, Emperor Hadrian wished to expunge all references to the Jews from this region, including the name they had used for their land. Consequently, he ceased using the name Judah for this territory and instead named it Provincia Syria Palaestina. That name was subsequently shortened to the Latin *Palaestina* or Palestine.[4]

Today, the modern state goes by the name of Israel. This name was given to the patriarch Jacob as a personal name (Genesis 32:28), and subsequently used to refer to the nation that derived from Jacob's gene pool. While it is not the most common name in the Bible for that area, there are several passages in the Old Testament that refer to the land on which this nation lived as Israel (1 Samuel 13:19; 1 Chronicles 22:2; Ezekiel 40:2). For centuries, those of Jewish descent composed a very small percentage of those living in the land, but following World War II, the Zionist Movement brought thousands of Jewish people to the area. They joined to form the modern state of Israel in 1948.

THE SIZE OF THE LAND

The borders of the Promised Land are discussed in several Bible passages. Nevertheless, precise drawing of borderlines is not always possible due to the gaps that exist in our geographical knowledge as well as the apparent contradictions that exist in border descriptions given in the Bible. For example, Numbers 34 implies that the borders of the Promised Land terminate at the Jordan River, while Joshua 12 and Ezekiel 47 imply that the Promised Land extended east of the Jordan River to the Syrian Desert, and included the territory from the Arnon River to Mount Hermon. Detailed discussion of these matters occurs in other sources,[5] so our purposes will best be served by describing the boundaries of the Promised Land in a more general way.

Perhaps the easiest way to describe the borders of the Promised Land is via the limits imposed by natural boundaries at every cardinal compass point. The northern boundary of Israel is formed by the Lebanon and Anti-Lebanon mountains. The southern boundary is the Wilderness of Zin and the Wadi el-Arish (River of Egypt). The western boundary of the Promised Land is the Mediterranean Sea. The eastern boundary is the Syrian Desert.[6]

When we define them as such, we are extending the borders of the Promised Land to the ultimate limit permitted by the biblical authors. Nevertheless, this still leaves us with a land that is significantly smaller than most envision. From north to south, the Promised Land measures approximately 200 miles. From east to west, the distance between the sea and desert varies between 80 and 105 miles (averaging 90 miles in width). These dimensions of the Promised Land describe an area of approximately 12,000 square miles. That description makes it about the same size as Maryland or Lake Erie, or one-fifth the size of Wisconsin or Missouri. Invariably, new visitors to Israel are struck by how much smaller the land is than they had anticipated.

The Diversity of the Land

Although this land is very small, it is a land with significant geographical diversity, as the photographs in the center of this book illustrate. Within the 200 miles of the northern and southern boundaries, one may experience every climate and ecological zone between sub-alpine and sub-tropical. We can walk in the snow among the pine forests of Mount Hermon, among the palm trees in Jericho, and past acacia trees in the desert of the Judean Wilderness. On the same day in August, the average high temperature at Jericho may be 102 degrees, while just 15 miles away in Jerusalem the temperature may be 75 degrees. One hundred miles to the north, snow may be gleaming on the fields of Mount Hermon. Mountain tundra, deserts, seashores, and marshy jungles are all part of the complex landscape that made up ancient Israel. Because being in one place in Israel is not like being in another, no single picture of the land will honor this great diversity in geography. To fully grasp the geography of Israel, we must compose a picture album that is filled with a great variety of images. As the readers turn the pages of their Bibles, they must also be ready to turn the pages in their picture albums. Even the story of Jesus, which occurs in a relatively small region, is set against a myriad of geographical settings. To fully appreciate the unique nature of each story, we must place it within its own unique geographical context.

We will begin to unpack this geographical diversity by dividing the Promised Land into four geographical zones: the coastal plain, the central mountain zone, the Jordan rift valley, and the eastern plateau. In the following paragraphs, a brief summary of each zone will prepare you to meet the more detailed descriptions offered in the following chapters.

The Coastal Plain

On the western side of the Promised Land we find a large plain with gently rolling hills. The coastal plain stretches 190 miles from Rosh HaNiqra in the north to the Wadi el-Arish in the south. The width of the plain varies from 50 yards to 15 miles, and grows wider and slightly higher in elevation as one travels south. The majority of this zone is an undulating plain with very low, rolling hills, most reaching no higher than 150 feet above sea level. As this region has a blanket of soil that has washed down from the central mountains, it is the most fertile of the zones and receives between 16 and 25 inches of annual precipitation. Standing in the heart of this plain, the traveler is overwhelmed not only by its fertility but also by its openness. The lower elevation of this gently rolling terrain favors international merchants and, in turn, the armies of empires who want to grow rich by taxing the merchants moving goods up and down the coast.

CENTRAL MOUNTAIN ZONE

Traveling east from the coastal plain, we meet the rising terrain of the central mountain zone. This zone extends through the heart of the country from Upper Galilee in the north to the foothills of the Negev in the south. The mountains of this region rise abruptly and dramatically, forming a sharp contrast with the coast to its west and the Jordan Valley to its east. Elevations in these mountains average between 1,500 and 3,000 feet above sea level, with many segments reaching over 3,300 feet. The mountains themselves are neither snowcapped nor forested, giving them a harsh and rocky appearance.

The degree of fertility and accessibility varies from north to south in the region. In general, the central mountain zone is the least fertile and least accessible of the four zones. It does not favor either the farmer or the international traders. The narrow valleys provide less surface area for planting and produce a much smaller harvest. The rugged mountains that rise above those valleys force north-south travelers onto exposed, undulating ridgelines. East-west travel through the zone becomes all but impossible at most places due to the topographic relief imposed by the mountains. In many places, an east-west trip inland would encounter up to five ridgelines, each separated by deeply cut valleys requiring thousands of feet in elevation change. Given the poor prospects for agriculture and trade, one may wonder who would want to live in this sort of place. The answer is simple: the individual wishing to live in the most secure portion of the country. International invaders rarely entered this zone due to its reduced economic value and rugged terrain.

JORDAN RIFT VALLEY

Traveling eastward from the Mediterranean sea, the third zone the traveler meets is the Jordan rift valley. And what a valley it is! This zone is part of the Afro-Arabian rift valley, one of the longest and deepest intrusions in the earth's surface. It extends over 4,000 miles from Turkey to the great lakes of Africa.[7] Within Israel, one can trace the primary fault line by following the streambed of the Jordan River. The valley begins at the base of Mount Hermon and follows the river during its 160-mile run, through the Sea of Galilee and to the southern end of the Dead Sea. This rift that primarily runs from north to south has also spawned a number of significant east-west valleys that radiate into the mountains. We will see that such valleys provide the easiest passage for travelers moving east and west through the central mountain zone.

Perhaps the most striking feature of this zone is its elevation. The great majority of the Jordan rift valley is below sea level. The surface of the Sea of Galilee lies at 700 feet below sea level. The surface of the Dead Sea is the lowest place on earth's surface at 1,300 feet below sea level. As one might expect, the effects of this deep, geologic scar in the crust of the earth makes its presence felt in more than one way. Within archaeological sites along the rift, there is clear evidence of devastating earthquakes that have reshaped the land and destroyed magnificent structures. Today, the Jordan rift valley still comes alive with brief tremors. While such tremors give occasional testimony to the geological dynamics of this valley, hot springs that dot the region offer a continuous reminder of the dynamic forces at work just beneath the surface. These springs, frequently visited by the ancient inhabitants for their soothing and healing qualities, are still used by modern visitors who feel the need for such a hot bath.

Fertility and accessibility vary greatly along the run of the Jordan rift valley. The northern portions of the valley are more fertile than those lying farther south, but even the more fertile portions of this zone are less desirable than the fields of the coastal plain. The Jordan rift valley is more accessible than the mountains lying either to its east or west, but travel and trade are made more difficult by the climate. The oppressive heat of the summer months, coupled with malaria-infested swamps, discourage significant travel through most of this region.

EASTERN PLATEAU

The eastern plateau, the final zone to be discussed, lies at the greatest distance from the Mediterranean Sea. The eastern plateau rises sharply and dramatically from the Jordan rift valley, forming a mountain-like facade.

It then levels off and tilts east, descending to the fringes of the Syrian Desert. This zone boasts mountain peaks that reach 5,000 feet above sea level. The dominant characteristic of the zone, however, is its plateau-like appearance. From the air, it presents itself as a high tableland that runs 250 miles from the base of Mount Hermon to the Gulf of Aqaba, varying in width from 30–80 miles. This tableland is incised by several deep canyons that carry runoff water from the mountains to the Jordan rift valley.

In the northern stretches, the fertility of this plateau rivals that of the coastal plain. But as one moves south, fertility begins to diminish. Eventually, the rainfall becomes so scarce that shepherding, rather than agriculture, dominates the economy. The plateau did favor north-south trade, but the route was less desirable than the one on the coastal plain due to the significant canyons one needed to cross east of the Jordan River.

The Plants and Animals of the Land

The tremendous diversity in geography presented in the four zones of Israel supports very diverse plant and animal communities within ancient Israel. By contrast to many of us living a more urban lifestyle, animals and plants would have been a regular part of people's lives during biblical times.[8] Today less than 2 percent of Americans are directly involved in agriculture,[9] while at the time of Jesus, 80 to 90 percent of the population was engaged in agricultural pursuits.[10] When we consider the fact that the animal and plant communities of Israel are likely to be very different than those regularly experienced by the readers of this book, we conclude that most of us have a lot to learn about this dimension of God's Promised Land. A detailed look at the flora and fauna of Israel lies outside the scope of this book, but we will take a few moments to introduce this fascinating dimension of God's Promised Land.

Plant life in Israel must find a way to cope with the unique rainfall cycle. Virtually all of the rain falls within 50 consecutive days in the winter, therefore plants have adopted various ways in which they adapt themselves to this cycle and the years of drought that they regularly encounter. Some plants increase their water intake through enlarged root systems, while others edit their physical growth to collect the summer dew more efficiently. Still other plants limit the amount of water they lose through transpiration "by developing thick and smaller leaves, reducing the number of stomata (openings for transpiration) and by acquiring a coating of wax, tiny hairs or thick, cork-like bark."[11] As plants vary in the degree and nature of adaptation, it is not unusual to find different forms of vegetation on opposing sides of the same hill—plants on one side enjoying a moist environment, while those on the other side have a drier environment.[12] Given these challenging growing conditions, one might expect there to be fewer plants. But, in fact, Solomon is said to have described the plant life of his kingdom in some detail (1 Kings 4:33). That is no small feat given that over 2,800 species of flowering plants alone grow in Israel.[13]

As people like Joshua or David walked the countryside, the principal forest cover they experienced was the maquis. The maquis is a cluster of plants comprised of various tree species (typically oak and terebinth) that grow no higher than about 15 feet. The trees grow very closely to one another creating a dense thicket at the base that is difficult to penetrate.[14] Today the impact of significant deforestation has robbed the land of its former appearance. This deforestation began in the biblical period as a product of agricultural clearing, denuding by flocks, and the use of wood during various wars.[15]

Domesticated plants also surrounded the people we know from our Bibles. Those plants played a key role in their lives by providing food, shelter, and income for the residents of the land. The Bible makes frequent reference to seven agricultural products expected from the land when the land was producing well. They are wheat, barley, grapes, olives, figs, pomegranates, and honey (Deuteronomy 8:8). We know that the diet of the Israelites also included various legumes and vegetables as well as cucumbers, watermelons, onions, leeks, and garlic.[16]

Wildlife is another dimension of God's creation that is rich and varied in the Promised Land. Over five hundred different species of birds have been observed in Israel, from the sparrow to the stork to the ostrich. Of those, 120 are migrants that are regularly observed during their migration season.[17] The ancient residents of Israel also had a chance to see reptiles and mammals that you may have only encountered in a zoo. This includes the hippo, crocodile, tortoise, gazelle, ibex, lion, bear, wolf, and cheetah.[18] Some of these animals became a food source for the people in this land, while others posed a threat to business and travel.

THE CHOSEN LAND

This land that is so unique in topography, flora, and fauna is God's chosen land. Before we leave this general introduction to Israel, let us pause for a moment to consider why the Lord would have choosen this land rather than another to be the Promised Land. Biblical authors repeatedly clarify that God created every acre of land on the earth's surface. The land of Israel was not the only land available to Him. So why would He choose this land rather than another? The inspired writers only hint at the answer. But by combining theology and geography we propose the following explanation. God chose Israel to be the land of hope because it was suited for proclaiming a message and because it inspired faith.

A Land Suited to Proclaim a Message

In order to better understand why this land is so powerful in proclaiming a message to the world, we first need to place it within the larger geographical context of the Fertile Crescent. The Fertile Crescent is a semicircle of land that extends from the Mediterranean Sea to the Persian Gulf. The north side of this arch is bound by that portion of the Alpine-Himalayan mountain chain known as the Taurus, Kurdistan, and Zargos Mountains. The south side of this arch terminates in the Arabian and Syrian Desert. Between the mountains and the desert is a relatively arable land. The more northern portions of this arch receive sufficient rain to grow grain. In the southern portions of this arch, water may be diverted by irrigation canals from the Tigris and Euphrates rivers to water the agricultural fields. In this arch between the rugged mountains and desiccating desert, the Fertile Crescent provided the natural resources needed to carry on life. The key here is water. If we take a map and mark the land watered by the Nile, the Tigris, and the Euphrates Rivers, as well as those areas receiving more than 12 inches of annual precipitation, we will have marked the Fertile Crescent.[19]

This arch is the home of the ancient Assyrian and Babylonian empires mentioned in the Old Testament. Among these more sophisticated people, we find the roots of modern culture that we take for granted. In this crescent, art, music, literature, and mathematics find their earliest recorded beginning. This is where humans "learned how to domesticate animals, to cultivate grains and become a food producer, to cluster dwellings and build cities and civilizations, to work metals, and to write."[20]

The Fertile Crescent was not only the seat of ancient culture but it was also the key to international transportation and trade. A highway that we will call the International Highway follows this arch. It courses through this arch for 1,770 miles from southern Egypt to the head of the Persian Gulf via a route between mountains and desert. Merchants traveled this highway buying and selling to everyone along the way. In the Promised Land this usable arch narrows to approximately 30 miles west of the Sea of Galilee. That makes Israel a land bridge from which the economy of the world could be controlled. It was this factor more than any other that consistently brought the larger empires of the Fertile Crescent to Israel. It became a tax station from which those empires could tax the goods carried by the merchants on the International Highway.

But that highway carried another commodity that the empires could not tax: the news of the day. If you had a message to deliver in the ancient world, you could either send messengers scurrying along the International Highway, or you could position yourself at a key point along that highway and speak a message that would be carried by others to the farthest reaches of the inhabited world. God did both. The apostles would travel this road, but even before they reached places well beyond the boundaries of Israel, the message of the Gospel had arrived ahead of them carried by other travelers on this ancient road. As the land of Israel is the crossroads linking Asia, Africa, and Europe, it becomes a podium.[21] Clearly one of the reasons that the Lord chose this land to be a stage for much biblical history was that the world would regularly come past this podium and carry what it heard to the farthest reaches of the world.

A Land that Inspires Faith

The second reason that God may have selected Israel as His chosen land is that it inspires faith in its residents. Faith is a quality highly praised by God in His message to us. As the psalmist says, "The LORD delights in those who fear Him, who put their hope in His unfailing love" (Psalm 147:11). God wants His people to turn to Him in faith. This quality is particularly desirable in the messengers who would speak from the podium in the Promised Land. They were to speak their message with faith and conviction. Israel is a land that inspires such faith. The messengers who live in this land do not live in comfort and security, but are harassed both by distant empires and local tribes. They live threatened by the Egyptian and Mesopotamian empires that bring their armies to ravage the land and control the international economy.[22] On only a few occasions in history have those who lived in this land actually controlled their own political destiny. Typically such autonomy only exists when the empires were weakened or distracted by other national and international events. The inhabitants of this land not only feared the empires but also the raiders that would sweep in from the desert at harvest time. "The desert dwellers are always half starved, and thus they gaze longingly at the delights of the settled country. They take advantage of every opportunity to invade the sown lands, requiring the frontier dwellers to be constantly on their guard."[23]

But perhaps the most significant factor that inspired faith in this land was the lack of Israel's natural resources compared to its neighbors. It possesses no gold and very few minerals.[24] But most significantly it is a land without an adequate supply of fresh water. The ancient inhabitants of Israel absolutely depended on rainfall to water their fields, fill their cisterns, and animate the springs. God promised to send that rain (Deuteronomy 11:13–15) and invited the people to put their faith in Him. Given the geographical realities of this land, it is clearly "a land that fostered faith."[25]

Why did the Lord select this land to be the Promised Land? The biblical writers do not lead us directly to the answer. But by combining what they do say with a sensitivity to the geography of Israel, we may propose that the Lord selected this land because it was an apt podium for the delivery of His message as well as a destitute land that invited the messengers in that podium to renew their faith in the Lord's promises.

3

THE COASTAL PLAIN

King Solomon was famous for two things: his great wisdom and his great wealth. Solomon's divinely inspired biographer reports, "King Solomon was greater in riches and wisdom than all the other kings of the earth" (1 Kings 10:23). The wisdom was a gift from God that would allow this young king to rule Israel with prudence and discretion. The wealth was also a gift from God. Have you ever paused to ask how it was that Solomon became so wealthy? Where did all the money come from? Part of the answer to that question lies in the region we are about to examine, the coastal plain.

In the pages that follow we will explore the topography, geology, hydrology, and natural resources unique to each of the sub-regions within Israel. The images we draw with words are complemented by the photographs in the center of the book and the maps at the beginning. Through the combination of words and images, we may construct our own mental map of each region, a map that includes key cities as well as impressions of the terrain, climate, and natural resources. Building on those impressions, this chapter and those that follow will explore the ways in which geography has directed history and shaped culture in that region. This, of course, will include key biblical events that illustrate how geography clarifies biblical texts and contributes to the process of their interpretation. As we begin our exploration of the coastal plain, we also begin our quest to answer the question raised above. How did geography contribute to the great wealth of King Solomon?

Boundaries and Dimensions

The coastal plain is the geographical zone that lies between the Mediterranean Sea and the foothills of the central mountain zone. In the north, the plain begins where a chalk ridge extends from Upper Galilee into the Mediterranean Sea. This steep, white ridge is called the "Ladder of Tyre" because one needed to climb it when traveling north from Israel to the city of Tyre. (This ridge is also referred to as Rosh HaNiqra, "head of the cave," because the sea has eroded cave-like channels beneath this promontory.)[1] As the plain moves south for 190 miles it expands and contracts in width as the mountains reach for and retreat from the sea. At its narrowest point near Mount Carmel it is merely 50 yards in width. Farther south the plain broadens to 20 miles in the vicinity of the Philistine Plain. The coastal plain eventually comes to an end at the Wadi el-Arish (River of Egypt). This seasonal riverbed drains most of the northern Sinai and enters the Mediterranean Sea at El-Arish.[2]

Topography, Geology, and Hydrology

As its name suggests, the coastal plain is a relatively flat portion of land extending along the Mediterranean Sea coast. In the immediate vicinity of the coast, this region is very level, but further inland it begins to roll with gentle hills that typically rise no more than 150 feet above sea level. The plain is interrupted in two places where the mountains dip their feet into the sea. The first is at the northern boundary of the plain where the Ladder of Tyre meets the sea. The second is approximately 20 miles south of this promontory where the Carmel ridge forms a bridge between the central mountain zone and the Mediterranean Sea.

The shoreline of the coastal plain is marked by sandy beaches and moving sand dunes. (See photo 1.) Some of these dunes have stabilized and hardened to form kurkar ridges. These ridges have a rock-like appearance that is produced when sand comes into contact with calcium-lime solutions. Despite their concrete-like appearance, they crumble easily but are resilient enough to block the intrusion of sand into the agricultural land lying immediately to the east.[3] These ridges vary in height from 30 to 100 feet, aligning themselves on a north-south axis parallel to the coast.

Moving east of the kurkar ridges, the openness and fertility of the coastal plain become evident. (See photo 2.) Annual precipitation of 12 to 28 inches is expected through the heart of the coastal plain with rainfall diminishing from north to south. Rainfall totals that are lower than that occur only at the extreme southern end of the plain. There the annual rainfall diminishes from 12 inches to 4 inches, which gives the plain an austere and desert-like appearance. But most of the plain is richer in water than the other zones due to adequate precipitation, a higher water table, and an abundance of springs.

The precipitation that falls in this zone meets two different types of soil in the wider segments of the plain. The western portion has sandy soil that is orange-red in color. This type of soil is particularly valuable for growing the citrus crops (including the Jaffa orange) in the Sharon Plain today. The eastern portions of the coastal plain are blanketed by the heavier alluvial soils, primarily terra rossa eroded from the central mountain zone.[4] This topsoil has accumulated for centuries and in places reaches a depth of 150 feet. The terra rossa soil is enjoyed by both wild and domesticated plants because it can hold water at a depth that plants can reach and enjoy during the driest season of the year. This combination of rainfall and soil makes the plain more lush and fertile than most other places in the Promised Land. This is the place to picture wheat and barley crops gently swaying in the breeze.

SUBDIVISIONS OF THE PLAIN

The Acco Plain

What at first glance from the air may appear as one plain will prove to be a series of smaller, individual plains divided by natural features. Each of these plains has its own name and unique characteristics. The northernmost segment of the coastal plain is called the Acco Plain. It stretches 13 miles from the Ladder of Tyre (Rosh HaNiqra) in the north to Mount Carmel in the south. The width of the plain is approximately 3 to 4 miles. The seaport city of Acco is often used to divide the Acco Plain into two smaller plains. North of the city of Acco, the plain is full of rich, alluvial soils that have washed down from Upper Galilee and have been watered by over 24 inches of annual precipitation. The absence of sand dunes along the coast means that field crops may be grown right to the edge of this well-drained plain.[5] South of the city Acco, the plain changes in character. This portion of the Acco plain is best characterized as a wide marsh.

The Na'aman and Kishon rivers empty their water into the Acco Bay within 6 miles of each other.[6] The movement of water toward the sea is hindered by kurkar ridges that block drainage, creating a high water table and marshy land. Despite its proximity to this marshy land, the city of Acco (later named Ptolemais) was an important ancient sea port because it provided access to a key road reaching into the interior of the country via the valley that flowed between Upper and Lower Galilee.[7]

The Dor Plain

Immediately to the south of the Acco Plain is the Dor Plain. This plain is cut off from the interior of the country by the ridge of Mount Carmel. That ridge stands like a wall forming the northern and eastern boundary of the Dor Plain. The plain extends 20 miles from Mount Carmel to the Crocodile River (Nahal Tanninim). Its width varies from a mere 50 yards at the base of Mount Carmel to 2 miles farther south. A quick look at a map might suggest that the Dor Plain is the most desirable way of traveling from the wider portions of the coastal plain northward toward Phoenicia. But this route is interrupted by rock outcroppings that slow the progress and increase the vulnerability of the traveler.[8] The narrow passage, thick forests, swamps, and Nile crocodiles that inhabited the river into the twentieth century provided more than enough discouragement for most travelers.

The Sharon Plain

Immediately south of the Dor Plain is the Sharon Plain. It extends from the Crocodile River in the north for 30 miles before terminating at the Yarkon River. The width of the plain is approximately 10 miles. In antiquity, nature conspired to make this a very inhospitable place, more often avoided than used. Two ingredients are necessary to create a bog: a high water table and poor drainage. The Sharon Plain has both. Mousterian red sand covers the surface 7 to 8 miles inland from the shore. This sand is very efficient at holding the groundwater just below the surface, and thus creates a very high water table. Three kurkar ridges near the coast block surface water from draining completely to the Mediterranean Sea. The soil and poor drainage turn the Sharon Plain into a thickly forested marsh.[9]

Ancient residents did not live on the plain proper but in the foothills on the eastern fringes of the plain. Below their homes, these residents looked down on a marsh filled with oak forests and thick scrub that remained largely untouched until World War I. But in this more hostile landscape, beauty is born. On the forest floor, the famed Rose of Sharon grew (Song of Songs 2:1–3). The red sand of this region provided the ideal growing conditions for this beautiful flower, but it did not favor the growing of grain.[10] Thus the region was largely untouched for agricultural purposes until more recently when the value of the soil for the citrus industry was discovered and the technology to drain the wetlands was in place. Today there is a thriving citrus industry in the region.[11] By contrast, the only specific use of this land mentioned in the Bible is grazing land for cattle (1 Chronicles 5:16 and 27:29).

The impassability of this forested marsh and the malaria easily contracted by those in its vicinity also shifted the travel patterns on the coastal plain. Travelers on the International Highway did not take the most direct route through the Sharon Plain, but detoured onto the foothills along its eastern side. The city of Aphek (called Antipatris in the New Testament) benefited from this pattern shift. Aphek was at the mouth of the Yarkon River with the foothills of the Judean Mountains lying just to the east. Resting in this gap between rising terrain and swamps, Aphek, with its shade and ample water supply, became a key rest stop for travelers along the International Highway.[12]

The Philistine Plain

The final segment of the coastal plain that we will consider is the Philistine Plain. This plain begins at the Yarkon River and extends 50 miles to the Nahal Besor, varying in width from 10 miles in the north to nearly 20 miles in the south. The lack of natural barriers allows sand dunes to intrude inland along the coast to a depth of up to 2 miles, particularly in the south.[13] East of the dunes in the central portion of the plain, terra rossa soil blankets the land. This soil, combined with 14 to 20 inches of annual precipitation, makes the heart of the Philistine Plain particularly suited for growing grain.

The great value and desirability of this agricultural land becomes clear only when we appreciate the critical role that wheat and barley play in the diet of the ancient inhabitants. These grains were the greatest source of protein and calories in their diet. Of the two, wheat contains a higher percentage of carbohydrates and proteins (60–80 percent carbohydrates and 8–15 percent proteins) making it the most desirable field crop. However, barley also had advantages. While it was less nutritional than wheat, it ripened earlier in the season and required less moisture.[14] Both of these grains were so critical to the diet of those living in biblical times that special steps were taken to guarantee a supply. In order to create a hedge against the loss of crops due to famine or military siege, a one-year supply was maintained by eating the grain harvested the previous season and placing the harvest from the current year into storage.[15] For that reason, agriculture was big business on the coastal plain. The combination of good soil and adequate rainfall promised a harvest that was ten to fifteen times the amount of grain sown. In order to reap the greatest possible harvest from their fields, the Philistines sought the aid of the grain god, Dagon. But the Bible demonstrates the futility of that worship when it reports the total collapse of Dagon before the ark of the covenant (1 Samuel 5:1–5).

The geography of the coastal plain not only favored agriculture, it also favored transportation in and through this area. This is one of the most open and accessible regions within Israel. There are no natural barriers either to trade or invading armies. Thus the Philistine plain opens Israel to the culture, influences, and armies of the world. Reading any historical account of this land will reveal that the residence of the Promised Land felt the threat or the burden of foreign invasion in almost every historical period, from the time of the ancient Egyptian empire to the days of the First World War.

The business world of the traders and the march of foreign armies lent significance to places such as Gaza that supported those traveling on the International Highway. Gaza, like most of the key cities on the plain, was located 3 miles inland to avoid the shifting sand dunes of the coast. Its abundant springs and position on the International Highway made it a critical staging and receiving point for travelers going to or coming from Egypt. This was the last significant oasis at which one could prepare for the eight-day trip south to the Nile delta. It was also the first major oasis one would encounter coming off the desert from Egypt, making it a temporary home for merchants and soldiers alike. George Smith calls it a "harbor for the wilderness and a market for the nomad."[16]

Maritime Commerce

A quick look at a map and the miles of coastline associated with the coastal plain would suggest that Israel would also be a land rich in sea ports and maritime commerce. By contrast to Phoenicia in the north, a country noted for its maritime culture, the Hebrew people never distinguished themselves in this way. Once again geography had something to say about that. First, the bed of the Mediterranean Sea slopes gently away from the coastline. The profile of the seabed is a product of the concordant shoreline and the sea currents that flow along the coast. As the mountains of Israel and the coastline of Israel are nearly parallel to each other, naturally occurring, deep-water ports are not present here. More so, the Mediterranean Longshore Current that flows counterclockwise from Gibraltar eastward along North Africa draws vast amounts of sand from Africa and deposits it along the shore of Israel, contributing to the formation of a shallow approach to the coast.[17] This means that seagoing vessels arriving on the coastal plain must unload their cargo onto smaller boats with shallower drafts for the trip to the docks.[18] Geography simply does not favor a maritime culture in Israel. "Thus, while the cruelty of many another wild coast is known by the wrecks of ships, the Syrian shore south of Carmel is strewn with the fiercer wreckage of harbours."[19]

Two of those harbors stand out when we consider biblical history. They are Joppa and Caesarea. Joppa appears as the primary seaport of the Hebrew people during the Old Testament. Here a small hill juts out into the Mediterranean Sea forming a protected bay. This is the seaport of Jerusalem. When Solomon transported logs from the forests of Lebanon for use in the temple at Jerusalem, he had those logs floated in rafts down the Mediterranean Sea to Joppa (2 Chronicles 2:16). From there it was uphill. Jerusalem lies 37 miles inland from Joppa at an altitude well above 2,000 feet, a climb that includes an ascent of nearly 800 feet up a 70 degree slope.

The seaport more closely connected to the history of the New Testament is Caesarea Maritima (referred to as "maritime Caesarea" to distinguish it from the Caesarea located near the base of Mount Hermon). This seaport was built by Herod the Great over the course of twelve years beginning in 22 BC and was named after his patron, Octavian Augustus Caesar. While giving the Romans a base in the region, it also served the interests of King Herod in a couple of ways. First, it was the city from which he could launch an escape to Rome. Herod was an astute politician who knew the risks of leadership in Israel. If things became too politically hot for him there, this port had a ship waiting to take him to Rome. Caesarea also was a way Herod could bring the culture and influence of Rome to Israel. He invested liberally in art, architecture, and social amenities that turned this seaport into a showcase of Roman culture by building a theater seating 4,000 patrons and an amphitheater seating 10,000 spectators. He was so successful in bringing Roman influence to Caesarea that the Jewish Talmud disparagingly called this city "the Daughter of Moab" (Megillah 6a), the Talmud's name for Rome. For conservative Jews it was an abomination, but for Herod it was a symbol of his wealth and a showcase for his ego, given that it was as large as the Athenian harbor at Piraeus.[20]

The harbor itself was 3.5 acres in size, composed of an arching breakwater 200 feet wide stretching 1/3 of a mile into the sea. This breakwater, constructed in 30 fathoms of water, protected the harbor both from sand intrusion and southwestern storms. By all accounts, it was the maritime engineering marvel of the day, and it required designers to solve construction problems they had not encountered before.[21] Caesarea was designed to be an international all-weather harbor, but it had no natural features to provide a starting point. There was no offshore island and no navigable river entering the sea, only a run of straight shoreline and an unstable sand foundation on which to place structures.[22] But at this most unlikely of spots is where a Roman port was built using hydraulic concrete for the first time in recorded history. The distinctive feature of this concrete is that it could be placed into water in a liquid state and harden there, achieving the same strength as concrete poured on dry land. What is even more striking about this concrete is its composition. Apparently the builders used Roman funds to provide volcanic sand called *pluvis puteolanus* from the Bay of Naples for the concrete mixture.[23]

Caesarea Maritima became a symbol of Rome's occupation of the land. It was the Roman capital from AD 6 and thus was the regular headquarters for Pontius Pilate (AD 26–36). Of course, most Bible readers will connect Pilate with Jerusalem. He was in Jerusalem at the time of Jesus' execution because Passover was a time when Jews of the first century thought more about their independence and a release from Roman authority. By leaving Caesarea Maritima and coming to Jerusalem, Pilate was making his own statement about Jewish freedom and the power of Rome he wielded in the region.

Despite the presence of harbors like Joppa and Caesarea, Israelite culture did little to exploit the commerce associated with the sea. There is also no evidence that they fished the waters of the Mediterranean Sea for seafood or that they harvested the murex shell like many of the other residents along the Mediterranean Sea.[24] The murex shell produced a deep purple dye, which was considered the finest dye in the ancient world. A robe colored by this dye might cost more than $10,000 and would be worn as a symbol of authority. Given that one shell might produce only a single drop of dye and that it would take 12,000 murex shells to produce 1.5 grams of dye,[25] it is no wonder that such garments were so highly regarded. Because such a unique garment was fit for royalty, it became a symbol of royal authority. Apparently such a garment was used by the soldiers as they mockingly dressed Jesus in a purple robe (Mark 15:17).

Biblical History

When all the geographical factors are entered into the equation, the coastal plain has the most desirable living conditions of all the regions in Israel. This is clearly the richest area in Israel and the most densely populated through most periods of history.[26] Ironically this is also the portion of Israel that sees the least amount of biblical history. The abundant water supply, rich agricultural fields, and money to be made from tax collection conspire to make this region a highly desired prize sought by the empires of the ancient world. And for most of the Old and New Testament period, someone other than the Israelites controlled it. During the time of the patriarchs, it was controlled by the Canaanites. During the time of the Judges, it was controlled by the Egyptians. During the time of the United Kingdom, the Philistines controlled it until David defeated them and placed the Israelites in control. After a brief stint in the hands of David and Solomon, the empires took possession. Assyria, Babylon, Persia, and Greece each took a turn milking the profits to be gained by taxing trade on the International Highway. Following another brief time of independence during the days of the Maccabees (164–63 BC), the coastal plain came under Roman domination where it stayed throughout the close of the New Testament period.

Although the region was desirable, the Israelites did not exert much presence or influence in the area. Consequently, we read very little in the Bible about events occurring here. If we read about the coastal plain, it is often in the context of the Philistines. The Philistines who dominated the coastal plain during much of the United Kingdom made their influence felt through five large city-states. We hear the most about those cities during the days of Samuel. When the Philistines were successful in capturing the ark of the covenant (1 Samuel 4), the ark traveled to several of those cities (1 Samuel 5) before being returned to the Israelites with an apologetic offering provided by each of the five city-states: Ashdod, Gaza, Ashkelon, Gath, and Ekron (1 Samuel 6:17).

During the time of David, the empires were distracted by other business, allowing David to gain control of the coastal plain. But it was his son, Solomon, who benefited most economically from this brief hiatus in the empire's control. Earlier, we raised the question about the source of Solomon's great wealth. As long as the United Kingdom of Israel could control the taxation system on the International Highway, millions of dollars in tax money poured into the royal coffers of Israel's king. That revenue from merchants and traders contributed significantly to the wealth of King Solomon (1 Kings 10:14).

The two seaport cities of the coastal plain are also mentioned in the biblical record. When Jonah was commissioned by the Lord to preach in Nineveh, he ran for the seaport of Joppa to sail westward away from his assigned mission field (Jonah 1:1–3). Centuries later, Peter raised the charitable Dorcas from death in the same seaport city (Acts 9:36–43). While Peter was in Joppa, the Lord invited him to leave this very Jewish city to preach the Gospel in the heathen metropolis of Caesarea Maritima. God used the vision of a large sheet filled with many kinds of animals to affirm for Peter that he must go to the home of Cornelius in Caesarea (Acts 10:10–20). Paul used the seaport of Ptolemais (Acco) when traveling from Greece back to Jerusalem (Acts 21:7). And Paul spent some time in Caesarea. Following his arrest in Jerusalem, Paul was in custody at Caesarea for more than two years standing trial before two Roman governors, both Felix and Festus (Acts 23–26). Of course, the person missing from this picture is Jesus Himself. Conspicuous by its absence is the ministry of Jesus on the coastal plain. For the most part, Jesus' ministry is spent in the central mountain zone where our attention will turn next.

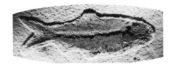

4

UPPER AND LOWER GALILEE

The region of Galilee provided the setting for Jesus' life prior to His public ministry. Although Mary and Joseph traveled to Bethlehem for His birth, they soon returned to their hometown of Nazareth. All indications are that this village remained Jesus' home, playground, and workplace throughout most of His life. The Gospel writers fall very silent in discussing the childhood and early adult life of Jesus in Nazareth. That silence also envelopes the decision of Mary and Joseph to live in Nazareth. What led them to select Nazareth as their home? The Gospel writers do not comment directly on this important decision, but once again geographical evidence suggests an answer to the question we have raised.

We will find that answer in the rising terrain that moves north and south through the center of the Promised Land called the central mountain zone. Here we find a series of interlocking mountain ranges that vary in elevation between 1,500 and 3,900 feet above sea level. In general, this region is higher in elevation than the coastal plain, more isolated from external influence, and less productive agriculturally. This zone with its dramatic, geographical diversity is the chief stage for biblical history. Given the importance of this zone for the Bible reader, separate chapters will be dedicated to present its geography. We begin with a closer look at the two sub-regions of the central mountain zone named Upper Galilee and Lower Galilee.

Although these regions share a common name, they are distinguished from one another in altitude, climate, vegetation, urbanization, and culture.[1] The name Galilee has been interpreted as "circle" or "district."[2] The designations "upper" and "lower" point to a marked difference in altitude between the two regions. Thus Upper Galilee is the district with higher mountains and Lower Galilee is the district with lower mountains. While no point in Lower Galilee exceeds 2,000 feet, the mountains of Upper Galilee are typically twice that high.[3] As this topographical difference produces very different cultural realities, we will discuss the two regions separately beginning with Upper Galilee.

Upper Galilee

Boundaries and Dimensions

Upper Galilee is 18 miles wide filling the void between the coastal plain on the west and the Jordan rift valley on the east. We place its northern boundary at the Litani River that flows from the base of the Lebanon Mountains. From there Upper Galilee stretches approximately 20 miles southward to the Beth Hakkerem Valley. On two sides, the boundary lines of Upper Galilee are marked by very steep mountain faces. On the east side of this region overlooking the Huleh Basin, the mountains drop off quickly, leaving near vertical faces that exceed 2,600 feet.[4] On the south side of Upper Galilee, the mountains form a 1,500 foot escarpment where they meet the Beth Hakkerem Valley, a valley that arches from the city of Acco to the north shore of the Sea of Galilee.

Topography, Geology, and Natural Resources

Upper Galilee is an extension of the Lebanon Mountains. It is high in altitude, rugged, and lush. The forces of nature guided by a divine hand have thrown the components of this region into strong relief. It is a maze of valleys, gorges, basins, ridges, and isolated peaks.[5] The more isolated and clearly defined peaks are found in the southern portion of this region. Here it is not uncommon to find summits reaching an elevation over 3,300 feet above sea level. As we travel north through this land of isolated peaks, we eventually find the landscape of Upper Galilee changing. While remaining high in elevation, the northern portions of Upper Galilee become more level, forming a high plateau that is cut by a spiderweb of fault lines running toward every point on the compass. This tableland slopes northward in the direction of the deep gorge that holds the water of the Litani River.[6]

The two most prominent features of the region are Mount Meron (Jebel Jarmak) and the Wadi 'Ammud. Mount Meron lies 12 miles northwest of the Sea of Galilee. The summit of this mountain resides at 3,963 feet above sea level, making it the highest point of land west of the Jordan River. The most prominent valley in the region is the Wadi 'Ammud. This deeply cut canyon drains into the Sea of Galilee and forms a barrier to traffic that wished to move north or south through the region.

The mountains of Upper Galilee are composed of hard limestone like most of the mountains in the central mountain zone. In the eastern section, we find Eocene limestone and occasional outcroppings of basalt. In the western portions, we find Cenomanian and Turonian limestone.[7] As the Cenomanian and Turonian limestone contains more silica and calcium, this limestone is very durable, eroding at a rate of just one centimeter per thousand years. The durability of this limestone makes it an excellent stone for the construction of buildings. Today we may visit structures used during biblical times that have survived the ravages of wind, water, and war because they were built from this durable stone. (See photo 27.) Eventually time does erode this limestone. The product of that erosion is a soil with a reddish hue, called terra rossa. (See photo 8.) The red-orange color of the soil is caused by the small amount of iron (10 percent) found in the parent rock.[8] This soil not only gives the landscape a pleasant tone, it also plays a very important role in keeping the native plants alive because it absorbs water easily and pays it out slowly during the dry summer months.[9]

When Edward Robinson traveled in this region during the second half of the nineteenth century, he described Upper Galilee as an "undulating tableland, arable and everywhere tilled with swelling hills in view all around covered with shrubs and trees."[10] This pre-modern description allows us to see the type of landscape that biblical characters would have observed in this region. The terra rossa soil on the plateau of Upper Galilee receives between 24 and 40 inches of annual precipitation each year. This creates a more lush setting in which the ancient residents could pursue agriculture and animal husbandry on the smaller plots of land the topography made available to them. (See photo 32.)

Various forms of wildlife were also drawn to this area, including the wild boar. The Bible does not mention them frequently because pork was removed from the Israelites' diet by divine command. But that dietary restriction did not prevent wild boars from enjoying this portion of the Promised Land (Psalm 80:13). These boars have an unassuming appearance boasting mottled coats with yellow stripes on a grey-brown background. They can weigh over 300 pounds and be as tall as the average person's waist.[11] Today, wild boars still inhabit the mountainous areas that are less settled. Modern hikers have very infrequent contact with them because they tend to be very shy and run away at the first sight or smell of humans. But watch out if they feel threatened because they will unleash brute force to make their point. A park services employee in Israel told the author of an incident where one of their park's department jeeps was overturned by a large boar who felt that the jeep was threatening his territorial rights.

Culture

The topography, geology, and natural resources of Upper Galilee had a clear impact on the culture within this region. The broken and dissected nature of the land conditioned the kind of settlement possible here. The residents of Upper Galilee lived on small, isolated farms. There is no evidence of a large urban center in Upper Galilee during the time of the Bible.[12] This is undoubtedly related to the difficulty associated with travel through this rugged region limiting the economic potential needed to foster such a city. (See photo 3.) The residents remained isolated from international influence and development as the major thoroughfares passed either to the east or west of Upper Galilee.[13]

Biblical History

The only significant biblical event that is associated with the region of Upper Galilee is mentioned in Joshua 11. A coalition of northern kings joined forces to resist the invasion of the Israelites at the Waters of Merom (near Mount Meron). It seems likely that this geographical setting had an impact on the outcome of the battle. The Canaanite forces had chariots with the capacity to devastate the Israelite infantry on level ground. Perhaps it was the rugged terrain and forests of this area that helped neutralize the strength and mobility of the Canaanite chariots, allowing for the great victory of the Israelites here.[14]

Lower Galilee

Boundaries and Dimensions

Lower Galilee lies immediately to the south of Upper Galilee. It covers an area that is approximately 15 miles long by 15 miles wide. The northern boundary is the Beth Hakkerem Valley where a rocky escarpment rises over 1,500 feet above the valley floor to form the dramatic break between Upper and Lower Galilee. The southern boundary is the Jezreel Valley. The eastern and western boundaries are the Jordan rift valley and the coastal plain respectively.

Topography, Geology, and Natural Resources

The most striking difference between Upper and Lower Galilee is the elevation of the mountains. While many summits in Upper Galilee extend well above 3,300 feet above sea level, no summit in Lower Galilee exceeds 2,000 feet. The story told by the altimeter is plainly evident to the eye. Lower Galilee is lower in elevation than its partner to the north.

As the character of Lower Galilee changes as one moves from west to east through the region, we will spend a few moments traveling laterally through the region to define those changes. After departing the coastal plain, the traveler first meets the foothills of northern Israel mentioned in Joshua 11:16. After moving up those moderately sloped hills, we meet the middle portion of Lower Galilee where a series of wider valleys are defined by mountain ridges of moderate elevation. While most of the mountains and valleys of Israel run north and south, the ridges and valleys of Lower Galilee are oriented east and west. When standing at the southern end of this region looking north, each ridge appears to rise a little above the next in elevation, climbing like a staircase toward the mountains of Upper Galilee. The elevation of these mountain ridges is much more modest than those found in Upper Galilee. For example, Mount Turan on the Turan Ridge rises to only 1,780 feet above sea level. Yet there is enough elevation change required by the repeated crossing of such ridges to discourage the north-south traveler from taking a direct route through the region.[15]

The farmers built their homes along the lower edge of these ridges in an effort to preserve the valuable farmland available. Within these open basins we find the largest, uninterrupted valleys in the central mountain zone. (See photo 4.) In this area, such valleys are the exception rather than the rule. That is why the ancient farmers were drawn to valleys like the Beth Netophah Valley that alone comprises 20 square miles. The basins of Lower Galilee are filled with terra rossa soil that has washed down from the ridges and are sated with 25 inches of annual precipitation. As George Smith traveled this region, he noted how distinctive it was from the rocky and dry appearance of Judah to the south. "The difference in this respect between Judea and Galilee is just the difference in their names. The one is liquid and musical like her running water, the other dry and dead like the fall of your horse's hoof on her blistered muffled rock."[16] As he rode his horse through this central region, Smith was struck by the profusion of brush and scattered oak forests on the ridges that rise above valleys filled with flowers and grasses.[17]

The easternmost portion of Lower Galilee can be identified by drawing a north-south line through Mount Tabor. While the mountain ridges west of this line orient themselves along an east-west axis, here the lines of relief turn southeast and northwest.[18] Although separated geologically from Upper Galilee, this portion of Lower Galilee continues the more rugged terrain we associate with the mountains of Upper Galilee. These mountains reach southward and plunge precipitously into the Sea of Galilee.[19] The eastern section of Lower Galilee also differs geologically from the central portion of this region. The Horns of Hattin, an extinct volcano cone, lies just a few miles west of the Sea of Galilee. This ancient volcano, the basalt rocks strewn about the hillsides, and the darker soils beneath those rocks all point to volcanic events that helped shape the character of eastern Lower Galilee.

Culture

The rich soils and plentiful rainfall conspire to make Lower Galilee a rich agricultural region. Grapes, wheat, and olives are the agricultural products that define Mediterranean dry farming and form the basic components of the human diet here.[20] In Lower Galilee, we find prime growing conditions for wheat and barley in the basins and for olive trees on the ridges. The olive tree is able to grow on very little soil, which makes it ideal for the ridges of this region where it would not compete with the grain crops growing in the basins.[21] To this day, visitors find olive trees on the ridges set in rows approximately 10 meters apart. Once mature, an olive tree could have a girth of up to 1.5 meters[22] and would bear olives every other year.[23] The olives harvested at the close of the summer from these trees found a variety of applications in society. Some were eaten whole while many were crushed to produce oil. The first pressing of the olives extracted the fine, virgin olive oil. Subsequent squeezing with a beam press produced oil of more inferior quality.[24] (See photo 30.) The oil functioned as a food source, as a fuel for lamps, as a medical treatment, as an application when anointing a person to public office, in worship rites, and in making soap and furniture.[25] Given the dry climate of Israel, olive oil also played a key role in preventing the drying and cracking of skin.[26]

The geography of Lower Galilee also favored one branch of the International Highway. We have seen that moving east and west through the central mountain zone was very difficult due to rising terrain that is oriented north and south in most of the country. But in Lower Galilee, the orientation of the rising terrain changed. The ridges and valleys of this region run east and west making east-west travel through the region much easier. The International Highway took advantage of this terrain orientation. It left the coastal plain and passed through the Mount Carmel range at Megiddo. After traversing the Jezreel Valley, the highway passed Mount Tabor and the Horns of Hattin before descending through the Arbel Pass to the Sea of Galilee. Where this highway traversed Lower Galilee, it brought with it the fortunes of international commerce and its attending international influence.

Biblical History

Bible readers typically have a greater interest in Lower Galilee than in Upper Galilee because it housed dramatic stories from Jesus' life in places like Nazareth and Cana. Nazareth takes pride of place because it was the home of Mary, Joseph, and Jesus. The hometown of this unique family was very small. The present archaeological investigation of Nazareth suggests that this village had a population of just a few hundred people, all of whom procured their drinking water from just one spring. When these individuals retired to their homes, they went to homes constructed so as to exploit the caves that formed naturally in the area. These caves were enlarged and covered with a facade that would shelter the living space from the elements. It was in such a home that the angel Gabriel announced to Mary that she would be the mother of the long-promised Messiah (Luke 1:26–38). Today a large basilica stands over the traditional site of the cave-home where this announcement took place. The present Basilica of the Annunciation was built in 1968 over the foundation of a twelfth century AD Crusader church. But archaeological evidence of a fourth century AD Byzantine church suggests that Christians were recalling this momentous event at this very location long before the Crusaders arrived.

Mary and Joseph left Nazareth so Jesus could be born in Bethlehem as promised in the Old Testament. But they eventually returned to live in this village of Nazareth. Some have suggested that Mary and Joseph lived here because it was near the city of Sepphoris.[27] Sepphoris rests on a hill above the Beth Netophah valley about 4 miles north of Nazareth. At this time, Herod Antipas was renovating Sepphoris so that it might become the capital of Galilee, the territory he was given after the death of his father. Because builders would be in demand, Joseph could have found steady work here. While this explanation of Mary and Joseph's residence in Nazareth is possible, there are a couple of problems with it. If Joseph had been looking for such work, Bethlehem offered him similar employment. Just a short distance from Bethlehem, the demand for workers on the unfinished Herodium would have coveted builders like Joseph. What is more, we have to wonder if Joseph would have felt comfortable working at Sepphoris. Of course, this city eventually became the place where the Jewish Mishnah was placed into writing in AD 200.[28] But this Jewish influence is not strongly evident at the time of Joseph. Herod Antipas was building a Roman city. This means Joseph would have worked on buildings and decorations that glorified the moral excess of Hellenistic life, a life that was contrary to all that conservative Judaism taught.

Because we have no evidence that Joseph actually worked in Sepphoris, we may entertain another reason for Mary and Joseph's residence in Nazareth. Perhaps it was the isolation and quietness of this small Jewish village that made it so desirable for Jesus' family. The first century saw the Jewish population lured again and again into the mindset and lifestyle of

Hellenism. Much of Hellenism stood in direct opposition to the will and intentions of God for His people. While some assimilated into the practices of Hellenism, others sought to isolate themselves from this worldview in small villages like Nazareth. It is precisely the isolation and insignificance of Nazareth that may well be reflected in John 1:46. Philip came to Nathanael to tell him about Jesus. But when Nathanael, who was from Lower Galilee, heard that his Savior was associated in some way with Nazareth, he was reluctant to believe it. He exclaimed, "Nazareth! Can anything good come from there?" (John 1:46).

Although Jesus lived His early life in Nazareth, this did not guarantee Him a warm homecoming when He returned later in life. After Jesus had initiated His public ministry, He preached and did miraculous acts that were near but not in Nazareth. The people of Nazareth had heard about this and thought that more of His energies should be directed toward His hometown. They became so upset with His claim to be the Messiah that they were ready to use the geography of the village against Him. They took Jesus to the precipice upon which the village sat in order to throw Him off (Luke 4:13–30).

Cana is another village mentioned in the Gospels. Cana lies approximately 8 miles northeast of Nazareth. This is the hometown of Nathanael (John 21:2) and the setting for Jesus' first miracle. Jesus and His family had been invited to a wedding celebration that ran into an unfortunate hitch: The wine had run out. Jesus' mother pressed upon Him to perform a miracle. He proved His heritage and His words to be true by turning water into wine in Cana (John 2:1–11).

5

SAMARIA

King David and King Solomon ruled the Promised Land as a united kingdom. From north to south, the land had one capital city and one king. But following the death of Solomon, the Promised Land split into two kingdoms with two different capitals and two different kings. The Lord challenged both kingdoms to advance the mission of salvation as His people. But the Northern Kingdom definitely had a problem remaining faithful to the Lord's calling. Why did the Northern Kingdom move away from the Lord more quickly and more dramatically than the Southern Kingdom? Several answers may be offered, but at least one is related to the geography of Samaria.

Biblical authors used a variety of names for the region we are about to study. In the Old Testament, this is the area settled by the descendants of Joseph's two sons, Manasseh and Ephraim. The Old Testament authors therefore named the northern segment of this region "Manasseh" and the southern segment "Ephraim." In the New Testament, the Samaritans lived in the area of Manasseh and Ephraim. Thus the Gospel writers refer to this region as "Samaria." As with other regions in the central mountain zone, Samaria provides the setting for many biblical stories. We will see how the investigation of its geography and culture sheds new light on stories like Elijah's contest with the prophets of Baal that occurred on Mount Carmel and on Jesus' meeting with the Samaritan women at the well in Sychar. And we will see how geography offers an answer to the question we raised above. During the time of the divided kingdom, why did the Northern Kingdom move away from the Lord more quickly and more dramatically than the Southern Kingdom?

Boundaries and Dimensions

The region of Samaria lies immediately south of the Jezreel Valley (discussed in the next chapter). The eastern border is the Jordan rift valley. The western border is the coastal plain and the southern border is marked by the Beth Horon Ridge and Wadi Makkuk that separates Ephraim from Benjamin. As the traveler moves south through the heart of Samaria (approximately 40 miles long and 35 miles in width), it becomes clear that this region provides a transition between Galilee to the north and Judah to the south. This transition is apparent in altitude, geography, and climate.[1]

Topography and Geology

When we look at Samaria from a distance, it appears to be a massive cluster of mountains. In reality, the topography of the countryside is much more complex, consisting of scattered mountain groups that are separated by small plains and open valleys. (See photo 6.) The topography of Samaria is constantly changing as one moves from west to east and north to south. A journey that begins on the western side of Samaria will first meet a series of uninterrupted ridges climbing steadily from the Sharon Plain.[2] A powerful hand has arranged the mountains into three parallel folds, each rising higher as one moves farther to the east with the eastern fold boasting the highest elevations.[3] There is also a change in topography as one travels from north to south. In general, the mountains increase in altitude from north to south while the valleys narrow between them. (See photo 9.)

Most of the mountains in this region and those to the south have a step-like appearance. While these steps appear to have been carved by human hands, they form naturally due to the composition of the mountains themselves. The majority of this mountainous terrain is composed of hard Cenomanian limestone. This limestone is subject to karstic dissolution. While this durable limestone is very resistant to wind and water erosion, it is very susceptible to chemical destruction. Carbon dioxide that is provided mainly by vegetation mixes with water seeping into the limestone. This solution initiates cracks that are widened and deepened by the roots of plants. Eventually these cracks compromise the face of the mountain so significantly that sections of rock will split off vertically in the same way that icebergs calve from glaciers. This produces the escarpments, steep slopes, and gorges that are typical of the central mountain zone. The horizontal steps that appear after the calving of the limestone are caused naturally by layers of marl interspersed horizontally between layers of limestone. This marl is not susceptible to karstic dissolution. Thus when the limestone blocks break off, they leave behind shelves or terraces that capture soil and provide a growing environment for the farmers in the region.[4] (See photo 6.) These steps may be enhanced by those farmers as they create terraces for their crops, but they form naturally due to the geologic composition of the mountains themselves.

Manasseh

The northern border of Manasseh is defined by the Mount Carmel Range that rises from the Jezreel Valley. A map easily shows how the 1,790 foot protrusion of Mount Carmel into the Mediterranean Sea would lead the ancient visitors to call it "the Antelope's Nose."

Mount Carmel

Mount Carmel proper skirts the shore of the sea for 20 miles. From there, this mountain becomes an extended ridge that stretches away from the Mediterranean Sea some 30 miles to the southeast. The sharply rising slopes of Mount Carmel capture precipitation and dew from the atmosphere and deliver it to the vegetation-laden hillsides. That vegetation includes the vineyards and olive groves that give rise to its name. Carmel means "plantation" or "garden-land."[5] The elevation of this mountain also has a dramatic impact on those wishing to travel north and south via the coastal plain. Given the arching turn that the Carmel Range makes from the Mediterranean Sea to the Dothan Valley, it provides the most significant barrier to north-south travel in the region. The first thought of a traveler might be to climb. But this is very difficult going due to the steep slopes and thick scrub forest that covers it. A nineteenth century traveler speaks about the difficulty he had in traversing this mountain.

> Ascending from the south, we followed a wild, narrow wadi overhung by trees, bushes, and tangled creepers, through which my guide thought we

could get up to the top, but it became absolutely impracticable, and we were obliged to find our way back again. And even after we reached the summit, it was so rough and broken in places, and the thorn bushes so thick set and sharp that our clothes were torn, and our hands and faces severely lacerated; nor could I see my guide at times ten steps ahead of me.[6]

The more desirable route is not over the summit but through passes created by naturally occurring Senonian chalk valleys. These valleys that lie perpendicular to the mountain ridge provide the most direct route through the Mount Carmel range. Furthermore, the chalk valleys tend to be lower in elevation, free of boulders, and quick to dry after a rain shower. The ease of travel in such valleys made it a natural place for the International Highway to run. Here is where we trace the footsteps of ancient traders and soldiers. And here is where we find large, significant cities forming in conjunction with these valleys that provide passage through the Mount Carmel range.[7] In the next chapter, we will see that one could literally control the international economy of the ancient world by controlling access to such valleys.

The Heartland of Manasseh

South of the Carmel Range lies the heartland of Manasseh. It stretches from the Dothan Valley and Mount Gilboa in the north to the Kanah Ravine (Joshua 17:7–10). This central section of Manasseh is a broad, uplifted basin with mountains on the edges. On the southeastern edge of Manasseh is where we see the distinctive combination of Mount Ebal (3,084 feet above sea level) and Mount Gerazim (2,891 feet above sea level). (See photo 8.) Within the mountains that rim the region, we find that the basin's soil is less fertile than that in Ephraim to the south.[8] Farther east in Manasseh, the rainfall shadow and outcroppings of chalk that overlook the Jordan rift valley conspire to give this mountain slope a more desert-like appearance. (See photo 7.)

Transportation through Manasseh is aided by lateral valleys that radiate from the Jordan rift valley. The most prominent wadi system is found in the south where the Wadi Shechem and Wadi Faria bisect the landscape. The traveler wishing to cross from the Jordan Valley to the Sharon Plain might well use these wadi systems as a roadway for this trip. The Wadi Faria makes a dramatic exit from the Jordan Valley at Adam on its way to Tirzah. Along the way it varies in width from one-half mile to nearly two miles traveling below sea level for most of its run.[9] This valley is a key passage into the interior of Manasseh because there is plenty of water and is easier to travel than routes over the mountains.

EPHRAIM

To the south of Manasseh lies Ephraim. A closer look at the geography of Ephraim shows that this region differs geographically from its companion region to the north. By contrast to Manasseh, the mountains of Ephraim are higher with steeper slopes leading to the summit. The mountains in this region are also closer together. This means that the valleys of Ephraim tend to be narrower and deeply cut into a V-shape. Both the terraces on the hillsides and the valley floors below are filled with the favorable terra rossa soil that provides a richer agricultural environment than in Manasseh.

Natural Resources

The average rainfall within Samaria (Manasseh and Ephraim) varies between 20 and 25 inches annually. But the topography of Samaria will cause local averages to vary. As the moist air masses leave the Mediterranean Sea and encounter the western face of Mount Carmel, they are forced upslope over 1,700 feet. Because the air at higher elevations is generally cooler and therefore able to carry less water, more significant rains can occur on the western side of rising terrain in Israel. That is why Mount Carmel exceeds the regional rainfall averages, boasting 32 inches of precipitation. This kind of rainfall produces a thick blanket of vegetation on its slopes. Thus when biblical authors speak about Mount Carmel, they often allude to its unique lushness (Song of Songs 7:5, Isaiah 35:1–2, Amos 1:2, and Micah 7:14).

The interior of Samaria gets less annual precipitation than Mount Carmel, but that moisture deeply affects the interior due to the land's topography. A number of significant valleys in Samaria are oriented along an east-west line. This provides a low-elevation opening to the west that allows moisture to permeate the interior. But ample rain does not penetrate all the way to the Jordan rift valley. On the far eastern side of Samaria a rainfall shadow is created east of the highest mountain ridges. Once the air masses have crossed this higher terrain, they have less water to offer the eastern slopes. The resulting lack of precipitation produces a 6-mile wide rainfall shadow. In this region that lies closest to the Jordan rift valley, the land sees only about 10 inches of annual precipitation, giving that belt of land along the Jordan rift valley a very dry and austere appearance.[10]

Culture

The geography of Samaria offered a life for the farmer, the shepherd, and the trader. The terraced hillsides and valleys of Manasseh and Ephraim would support the cultivation of grain, grapes, and olives. Adequate rainfall and adequate food supplies combined to support significant urbanization here. The businessperson also benefited from the greater openness of the land because the transportation of goods was always less expensive when the fight with gravity was reduced. But this accessible topography was a double-edged sword for the residents. The geography of Manasseh, in particular, created opportunities to trade goods with the world. But along with the benefit of trade also comes the risk of ideological and military invasion. Samaria was frequently visited by both.

Biblical History

Therein lies the answer to the question we had raised earlier regarding the apostasy of the Northern Kingdom. Manasseh lies at the core of the Northern Kingdom, that part of King David and Solomon's Israel that split off during the civil war following Solomon's death. The biblical writers frequently refer to the way that the Northern Kingdom of Israel abandoned the Lord to follow alternative religious ideologies twisted by the invasion of foreign gods and goddesses. The openness of the terrain made it easier for trade and alternate ideology to reach this land. By contrast, the Southern Kingdom was more isolated from ideological invasion due to its geography. This difference in geography contributed to the more rapid apostasy of the Northern Kingdom of Israel. And when the Lord's patience grew thin with this apostasy, the open terrain of the Northern Kingdom allowed Assyria to quickly and easily invade Manasseh and Ephraim, taking its population into captivity.

The region of Samaria provides the setting for a number of additional familiar Bible stories. The distinctive lushness of Mount Carmel led many ancients to regard this mountain as a sacred spot. As early as the fifteenth century BC, the Egyptians called this mountain "Holy Headland."[11] Perhaps then, it is no surprise that Mount Carmel served as the stage for one of the most dramatic duels recorded in the Bible, the duel between Elijah and the prophets of Baal. Baal was the deity to whom the Canaanites turned for life-giving rain. The Israelites often struggled with the assimilation of Baal worship from the time that they arrived in the land. But things took a dramatic turn during the days of Ahab and Jezebel. During their time as leaders, the worship of Baal became an official part of the culture in the Northern Kingdom when King Ahab built a temple for Baal in his capital, Samaria (1 Kings 16:32). In an ironic twist, the Lord imposed a famine on the land whose residents were being won for the rain god. In 1 Kings 18, Elijah is sent to challenge the 450 prophets of Baal to a duel. The god who would produce rain when it was requested would prove himself to be the one true God. It is worth noting that this contest occurred on the very fertile flanks of Mount Carmel, which Baal worshipers had adopted as a key worship site. Baal was a god of rain and this mountain experienced significant amounts of rain. Thus, when Elijah met the 450 prophets of Baal on Mount Carmel, not only was he outnumbered but he was also playing on the opposition's "home field."[12] This amplifies the message of the victory. For if Baal could not prove himself on this mountain, he would not be able to prove himself anywhere.

Shiloh, 20 miles northeast of Jerusalem, makes a more humble appearance on the pages of the Old Testament. Joshua gathered the Israelites here after the conquest of the land in order to finish dividing the land among the twelve tribes (Joshua 18:1). This meant that every single family of Israel received a piece of land that God had promised them. This was their personal reassurance that God would keep all of His promises—including the one to provide a Messiah who would be born on this land. The rugged terrain of Ephraim that surrounded Shiloh was hard to penetrate. This made it the ideal home for the Israelite sanctuary and the ark of the covenant. During the period of the Judges and early days of Samuel, the Israelites went here to worship (Judges 18:31 and 1 Samuel 1:3). But when the Israelites attempted to use the ark of the covenant improperly by taking it into the Battle of Aphek (1 Samuel 4:1–11), it was lost to the Philistines. Apparently the Philistines continued their military penetration all the way to Shiloh and destroyed the sanctuary there (Jeremiah 7:12).

King Omri selected a 300-foot hill that rises above its wide basin for the capital of the Northern Kingdom, Samaria, in 876 BC (1 Kings 16:23–24). The summit extends over 50 acres, and provides both the room and security that the earlier capitals of Shechem and Tirza lacked. It was in the palace built here that we trace the footsteps and missteps of King Ahab and Queen Jezebel as they leave their dark mark on the history of God's people. Their apostasy continued a wave of disaffection among the people that eventually would lead to the destruction of the city by the Assyrians and the exile of the ten northern tribes in 722 BC (Hosea 10:5–7).

In the New Testament, Samaria becomes the city of Sebaste. But in an ironic twist of fate, this city with the new name is inhabited by another evil king. King Herod the Great built a palace here and a large temple that he dedicated to Augustus, the Roman emperor. Behind the wall of this palace, Herod found respite from the Jews who opposed him, as well as ready access to the seaport of Caesarea. On a clear day, it is possible to see the Mediterranean Sea from the steps of the temple. If the political situation grew too dangerous for Herod, he would be able to travel 20 miles downhill to his seaport of Caesarea and flee to Rome aboard one of the ships kept there.

The modern city of Nablus was also the scene of many biblical events. The contemporary city surrounds the area that was once the Old Testament city of Shechem. Shechem lies right at the heart of the central mountain zone in Israel and may be regarded as a transportation hub. From here, roadways radiate out toward Beth Shan and Samaria to the north, Jerusalem to the south, the coastal plain on the west, and to a key Jordan River ford leading to the eastern plateau in the east. The importance of this city in antiquity is witnessed both by its early settlement and its mention in the Bible.

As Moses relates the story of Abram, Shechem is the very first city Abram visits after entering the Promised Land (Genesis 12:6). Its strategic position and fertile fields made it a key city in this land over a millennium before Abram's visit. But from the moment Abram arrived here and was told that this land was to be his home and the stage for the divine rescue plan, Shechem became a focal point for biblical events. When the children of Israel brought the bones of Joseph back from Egypt, they were interred here at Shechem (Joshua 24:32). Then Joshua placed the people between

Mount Ebal and Mount Gerazim for a service of worship and rededication to the Lord before they continued the conquest of the Promised Land (Joshua 8:30–35). Once that conquest was completed, Joshua brought the people back to Shechem for a second service of worship and rededication (Joshua 24). He challenged them to remain faithful to the Mosaic Covenant with the stirring plea: "[C]hoose for yourselves this day whom you will serve . . . But as for me and my household, we will serve the LORD" (Joshua 24:15). Thus, both the promises given to Abraham and the agreement made with Israel through Moses give the city a theological history that elevated it above others in importance. The religious sentiments associated with Shechem led Rehoboam, Solomon's son, to seek coronation on this very spot (1 Kings 12). While this bid for kingship of all Israel was not successful, another less assuming King comes to this city.

By the time of the New Testament, Shechem had become Sychar. It was here that Jesus visited with the Samaritan woman at the well and did something He apparently did very infrequently during His earthly ministry. The Gospel writers rarely record Jesus saying in so many words that He is the Messiah, yet He does so here. As Jesus sat by Jacob's well, He met and spoke with a Samaritan woman who had come out to draw water. (See photo 10.) The Samaritans were not 100 percent Jewish either in their bloodlines or in their theology. But they did maintain a theology that was roughly formed around the Pentateuch, building their own temple on top of Mount Gerazim. Although John Hyrcancus destroyed that temple in 128 BC, Samaritans still worshiped on the site at the time of Jesus as they do today. As Jesus addresses the Samaritan woman's confusion about Jewish and Samaritan theology, she responds, "I know that Messiah (called Christ) is coming. When He comes, He will explain everything to us." Jesus responds immediately by saying, "I who speak to you am He" (John 4:25–26).

Given how infrequently Jesus declares Himself as Messiah, why does He do so here? It may be because of the theological promises connected to this site. Here Abram first builds an altar after being promised that his family would become a great nation, live on this land, and produce a child who would be the promised Messiah. Here Joshua leads the Israelites in rededicating themselves to God's plan for the nation that would bring the Messiah into the world. And here, in a spot so rich in the history of this promise, Jesus claims to be the One. Given the geographical significance of Shechem, it is hard to believe this revelation is serendipitous. We argue that this is no accident but the strategic preaching of a message at a critical geographical location. By selecting this spot for this announcement, Jesus proclaims Himself to be the fulfillment of all the promises of Messiah previously connected to this site.

6

JEZREEL VALLEY AND BENJAMIN

J oshua instructed the people to arm themselves and march around the
city of Jericho just once before returning to camp for the day. This
strange military assault was repeated for six days. On the seventh day,
Joshua ordered the people to march around the city seven times. During
the seventh circuit, when the people heard the priests blowing the trumpets, they shouted and the walls of Jericho fell (Joshua 6). The details of
Jericho's fall may be well known to you, but do you know why Joshua
chose to invade the Promised Land through the corridor that led past
Jericho? What made this relatively small Canaanite outpost the first target
in a massive military strike against the land? Once again, an awareness of
geography will help us answer those questions as we learn more about the
Jezreel Valley and Benjamin.

The rising terrain of the central mountain zone provides the ancient
traveler with beautiful scenery and challenging obstacles. Because the
mountains that move through the center of the country generally align
themselves on a north-south axis, the traveler moving east and west must
climb and descend through a series of valleys and ridgelines. In some
places, a single climb and descent between ridgelines may mean an elevation change of over a mile. As most travelers in the biblical period would
be traveling on foot, they would personally feel the thousands of feet in
altitude change that mark an east-west crossing of the Promised Land.
Consequently, they would look for places to cross where the net elevation

change was less dramatic. And that is where the Jezreel Valley and Benjamin come into play.

Although they do not lie adjacent to each other, we have elected to treat the Jezreel Valley (called the Esdraelon Valley in the New Testament) and Benjamin together because they are both interruptions in the central mountain zone. As suggested by its name, the Jezreel Valley is a wide valley that breaks through the mountains allowing the east-west traveler to cross with only several hundred feet of elevation change. The tribal territory of Benjamin is an interruption of a different kind. The western portion of Benjamin is not a valley but a high plateau. While the east-west crossing of this plateau demands more elevation change than that of a valley, it is still less arduous than a crossing through the mountains immediately to the north or south. Thus it becomes a more popular east-west travel artery as well. We will now explore both regions in more detail while keeping in mind the similar roles they play for the ancient travelers.

Jezreel Valley

Boundaries and Dimensions

From the air, the Jezreel Valley has the appearance of an equilateral triangle with each leg extending approximately 20 miles. (See photo 5.) The points of the triangle take aim at modern Haifa in the west, Ibleam in the south, and Mount Tabor in the north. The southern leg of the triangle is formed by the Mount Carmel Range and Mount Gilboa. The northern leg is drawn by the Nazareth Ridge and hills of Lower Galilee. In the east, rising terrain curls around the north and south corners of the triangle forming an eastern leg to the triangle. These mountains in the east threaten to touch and close off passage to the Jordan River Valley. But it is at this point that the narrow Harod Valley leaves the larger Jezreel Valley and continues its journey to the Jordan Valley. The Harod Valley extends 11 miles from the city of Jezreel to Beth Shan where it meets the Jordan River just 14 miles south of the Sea of Galilee. This ribbon of land is narrow, achieving a maximum width of only 3 miles, whereas the Jezreel Valley widens to over 18 miles. When we combine the two valleys on our map, they have the appearance of an arrowhead (Jezreel Valley) and shaft (Harod Valley) that provide a geographically appealing route from the coastal plain to the Jordan Valley.

Topography and Geology

When standing in the middle of the Jezreel Valley, its unique topography becomes apparent. All around, the mountains rise above the observer in the center of a gently undulating plain rising only slightly above sea level. The highest portion of the Jezreel Valley resides at a mere 160 feet above sea level before sloping toward the Mediterranean Sea and the Jordan River. A glance in the direction of Mount Tabor that rises 1,843 feet above sea level and Mount Carmel rising 1,790 feet above sea level helps put the elevation of this valley into perspective. Given the contrast of the mountains rising on all sides, one hardly notices that the valley itself is divided into two basins by a bridge of basalt that extends from Megiddo to Mount Tabor. But, as we shall see, this slight rise in terrain will be important to ancient travelers when the valley becomes clogged with excess water.

The valley floor is filled with alluvial soils. In a few places, the soil takes on a red-orange appearance signaling the presence of terra rossa soil. But most of the valley floor is filled with black topsoil derived from its basaltic, parent rock in Galilee. Mount Moreh, an extinct volcano cone that lies within the valley itself,[1] also made its contribution to the valley floor leaving places around Megiddo with topsoil that exceeds 330 feet in depth.[2] This soil is dark, heavy, and rich in organic matter due to the swamps that existed here in antiquity.[3]

Natural Resources

Because the Jezreel Valley is surrounded by hills, we might expect that it would have very little annual precipitation. But the rainfall shadow is only a partial shadow due to the geography of Manasseh to the south. As the rising terrain of Manasseh opens a corridor to the southwest, rain-bearing winds are able to move into the Jezreel Valley more easily.[4] The western portions of the valley receive over 20 inches of precipitation. This diminishes to little more than 12 inches near Beth Shan. A small portion of this water is drained to the Jordan River via the Harod Valley. But a more substantial amount of this region drains to the west via the Kishon River. This river begins at the base of Mout Gilboa and travels west through the Jezreel Valley before exiting into the coastal plain through the narrow opening between the slopes of Mount Carmel and the Shefar'am Hills of Lower Galilee. Because this opening is little more than 100 yards wide, a significant rainstorm can cause the small river to swell, back up, and flood the plain. At other times, the river may be lost to the casual observer because it is little more than a muddy trench carrying a small rivulet of water. William Thomson, a nineteenth-century explorer, reports: "The first time I crossed the Kishon in a boat and swam the horses; the next time there was no river at all, not even a rill to be seen."[5]

Culture

As in other regions, geography plays a significant role in shaping the cultural use of this valley. The name Jezreel is a Hebrew word that means "may God sow." The combination of rich soil and moisture means that the Jezreel Valley was uniquely designed to produce rich harvests of wheat. While the ancient farmers would have plowed and planted this very valley, their harvests may not have been as spectacular as today's due to the high water table and flooding of the valley floor.

An even richer reward offered by this valley was ease of movement. The Jezreel Valley provided the most convenient east-west route through the central mountains because it offered the traveler the most level grades that minimized the net elevation change. That is why the International Highway that connected Asia, Africa, and Europe moved through this valley. It is also why the empires of the world wanted control of this valley. If one wished to tax and control international trade, this was the place to do it. For this reason, the Jezreel Valley became a regular battleground for those intending to control the international economy.

That control was realized by establishing cities at key points of access to the valley. Taxes were extracted from the international merchants, in effect charging them a toll for using the valley floor. Several of those gateways merit mention. International travelers moving north on the coastal plain would have their forward progress blocked by the imposing rise of Mount Carmel. This forced the travelers to abandon the valleys for travel up narrower mountain passes that pressed through Mount Carmel to the Jezreel Valley. The most desirable pass is a chalk valley that moves from Aruna to Megiddo via the Wadi 'Iron. (Alternative routes included taking the less direct or more difficult routes via Taanach or Ibleam.) International travelers would typically leave the coastal plain and travel to Megiddo via the Aruna Pass. From Megiddo they traveled east, skirting the slopes of Mount Carmel in their approach to the city of Jezreel and the Harod Valley. An alternate route also started at Megiddo, traveled across the Jezreel Valley on the basalt causeway that leads in the direction of Mount Tabor, and then climbed into the valleys of Lower Galilee on their way north. Given its location, Megiddo becomes the most critical city in Israel for controlling international trade income. Other gates played a secondary role. Jokneam guards a pass that connects the Dor plain with the western portion of the Jezreel Valley. Access on the eastern size of this valley system is controlled by the cities of Jezreel and Beth Shan. Beth Shan's position is particularly strategic because it resides at the crossroads of the Jordan Valley and the Jezreel-Harod Valley immediately opposite a key ford in the Jordan River.[6]

These access points to the Jezreel Valley became the focus of international interest as the superpowers of the ancient world looked to fill their pockets with trade revenue. This also makes the Jezreel Valley and its associated gates the frequent scene of international battles. The likes of Thutmose III, Alexander the Great, and Napoleon have all participated in battles for control of this critical piece of land. Perhaps it is not surprising that when John wrote about the final battle that this world would see in Revelation 16:16, he spoke about the powers of the world gathering at Armageddon. This is in fact a Hebrew expression that may be translated, "the Mountain of Megiddo." The powers of the world have been invited to do battle against the people of God by demonic spirits. The stakes of the battle will be so high and the battle so fierce that the Holy Spirit leads John to associate this battle symbolically with the Jezreel Valley, for no portion of Israel had seen the kind of battles in history that this valley had seen.

Biblical History

Given the strategic significance of this valley, it will be no surprise to read about its role in biblical history. We have seen that to control Megiddo is to control the world's economy. Its nearly continuous occupation from 3,500 BC to 350 BC by many different nations gives witness that this is the most strategic location in Israel.[7] For example, it was of vital importance to the Egyptian pharaoh, Thutmose III (ca. 1490–1436 BC). During his reign in Egypt, he led annual campaigns into the Promised Land for nearly twenty years. In the Temple at Karnak, we can read about his attack on Megiddo using a plan that involved a very risky approach via the Aruna Pass. It was the most direct and easiest route to attack Megiddo from the south, but it became so narrow in places that horses needed to walk single file. There is simply no way to maintain security in this situation. If the lead units were engaged in battle, the rear units would be geographically cut off from offering them any sort of aid. The opposition assumed that the Egyptians would not make such a risky move and left this pass unguarded. The risky Egyptian strategy caught the enemy completely off guard. The leaders fled to Megiddo hoping in vain that the walls would protect them from the Egyptian army. As the city came under siege, Thutmose III gave the following instructions to his generals, "Capture and fortify this city well. For the capturing of Megiddo is the capturing of a thousand towns!"[8]

Solomon appreciated the tenor of these words. As he consolidated his nation, Megiddo was among the cities he fortified (1 Kings 9:15). Somewhat later in history, another Judean king was mortally wounded near Megiddo. Pharaoh Neco of Egypt was on his way to assist the Assyrians in a battle at Carchemish that would change the balance of power in the ancient world. King Josiah of Judah wanted to prevent Neco from participating in this battle, so he engaged the Egyptian army as they moved up the International Highway near Megiddo. The Egyptians and Assyrians went on to lose the battle to Babylon. But on their way, they also ended the life of the last reforming king to sit on Judah's throne before the Babylonian captivity (2 Kings 23:29–30).

Earlier, another Israelite king perished in a battle for control of this valley and its eastern gate, the city of Beth Shan. King Saul's last battle against the Philistines was a battle for the control of this region. The battle was a rousing defeat for the Israelites. And after Saul was mortally wounded, he took his own life on Mount Gilboa. When the Philistines found his body, they took it as a trophy of war and hung it on the wall at Beth Shan (1 Samuel 31).

The Jezreel Valley was also the scene for a battle between Israel and Jabin, King of Hazor (Judges 4). Deborah was dispatched to deliver the battle plan for this fight to Israel's general, Barak. The plan demanded an extra measure of trust from Barak because he was told to muster his forces on Mount Tabor. This mountain rises 1,843 feet above the Jezreel Valley and was the ideal place for the infantry of Israel to neutralize the chariot forces of Hazor. It provided the advantage of being above the attackers while at the same time frustrating any sort of chariot attack against them.[9]

It was not surprising to Barak that the troops should muster and fight at Mount Tabor. But what was absolutely shocking is that they should leave and make a frontal charge on the Canaanite chariots in the plain! This plan called for an unqualified faith in Barak. But he hesitated, and his lack of faith in God's plan cost him the honor of the victory (Judges 4:9).

Yet another battle occurs in this valley during the days of Gideon. This time the enemy comes from Midian. The Midianites had encamped on Mount Moreh. Gideon and his troops were camped at the Harod Spring. The Lord wanted to be sure that He received full credit for the victory that was about to occur in the Jezreel Valley, so He used various means, including the way in which the soldiers drank from the spring, to reduce the fighting force to 300 men (Judges 7).

Jesus Himself would have spent time in and along the Jezreel Valley. And one dramatic moment from His life is traditionally set on the summit of Mount Tabor. On the top of this mountain today we find the beautiful Church of the Transfiguration that commemorates that monumental moment in Jesus' life. Christians visited this location as early as the fourth century proclaiming it the location of Jesus' transfiguration. Pilgrims traveling to Nazareth to visit the Church of the Annunciation would have relished the short walk to Mount Tabor where they could honor another significant event in Jesus' life. But there is some question as to whether or not Mount Tabor is the "high mountain" (Matthew 17:1) on which this event occurred. Even during the Byzantine period, the debate demanded consideration of Mount Hermon and the Mount of Olives as well as Mount Tabor.[10] Thus while we may be sure that Jesus walked the valley near Mount Tabor, the exact location of His transfiguration remains uncertain.

BENJAMIN

Boundaries and Dimensions

The second best route to use when traveling from east to west through the central mountain zone is the route associated with the tribal territory of Benjamin. Benjamin resides between the mountains of Ephraim and Judah, extending approximately 14 miles from north to south and 27 miles from east to west. The northern border begins at the Jordan River and extends through Bethel before turning southwest to Lower Beth

Horon. The southern border follows the Wadi Qilt traveling just north of Jerusalem on the way to Kiriath Jearim.

Topography and Geology

The central and western portions of Benjamin resemble a high plateau (2,500 feet above sea level) whose most prominent feature is Nabi Samuel at an elevation of 2,942 feet. This plateau is not completely flat but rolls with hills of varying size and dimension. (See photo 11.) In the east, the high plateau turns into rugged desert as it takes on the characteristics of the chalk mountains in the Judean Wilderness. In the west, the Beth Horon ridge descends from the plateau to the Aijalon Valley. This ridge became an important travel artery because the deeply eroded valleys on either side of this ridge discourage the use of alternate routes.[11]

Culture

The plateau area of Benjamin receives 25 inches of precipitation that mixes with the agriculturally productive terra rossa soil. Combined, they give birth to the productive fields in which Saul was plowing when he received the plea for help from Jabesh Gilead (1 Samuel 11:5). But this plateau played a far more critical role as a transportation artery across the mountains. The traveler could leave the coastal plain via the Aijalon Valley, climb the Beth Horon Ridge, cross the Benjamin plateau, and continue east to Jericho and the Jordan Valley. As this road did require several thousand feet of elevation change, it did not rival the Jezreel Valley for the attention of international traders. But it was the key east-west transportation route for those living in the hill country. Because the north-south road that traveled on the ridge from the Negev to the Jezreel Valley also passed through this plateau, Benjamin became the key internal crossroads of the country. Anyone wishing to control the central mountain zone of the Promised Land would need to control the plateau area of Benjamin. Thus when we see international powers leveling their attention on Jerusalem, we can be assured that they will follow the typical attack route leading from the coastal plain to Jerusalem via the Benjamin plateau.[12] This predictable route motivated the residents living in the hill country to establish protective fortifications on either side of Benjamin. On the western side of this plateau, we find the defensive cities, Upper and Lower Beth Horon. Because invasion from the east was also a potential threat, the city of Jericho was established as the eastern border fortress. This oasis in the desert stood opposite a key ford that crossed the Jordan River. Thus Jericho stands like a sentry guarding access to the roads that lead to the strategic Benjamin plateau in the interior of the country.

Biblical History

As we read the Book of Joshua with sensitivity to geography, the divine plan for invading the Promised Land becomes clear. Jericho would be the first fortification to feel the pressure of Joshua's army (Joshua 6). It is not the size of this fortification that makes it so critical. In fact, Jericho is quite average in size covering only 8.5 acres. It is the strategic position of Jericho as the guardian of the road west into Benjamin that makes it the first target. Once that site has been neutralized by the hand of God, we read about the successive battles and negotiations with Ai, Bethel, and Gibeon, all cities associated with Benjamin. Thus the strategy of Joshua is clear. The targets for this military assault are not chosen haphazardly. First, the gate at Jericho will be neutralized and eliminated as a threat to his supply line stretching to the east side of the Jordan. Next, Joshua will divide the country in half while capturing the key internal crossroads of the country.

Once this strategy began to take shape, the leaders of Gibeon recognized that Joshua's plan would soon put them directly in the crosshairs of the Israelite army. Because Gibeon lies a mere 15 miles west of Jericho, they immediately dispatched a delegation to draft a non-aggression pact with the Israelites. In order to make their case more convincing, they pretended to be from a distant country by displaying worn out clothing and gear. The Israelites were taken in by the ruse and consequently the Canaanite city of Gibeon was spared (Joshua 9).

Gibeon lived on to surface again in two other important Bible stories. After the death of Israel's first king, King Saul, a civil war broke out that pitted the descendants of Saul against David. The only recorded battle of that seven-year civil war is the one that occurs at Gibeon (2 Samuel 2:12–16). Although other battles were fought during this civil war, the one regarded most noteworthy is the battle over the city standing at the crossroads of the central mountain zone. Later David's son makes an appearance in Gibeon. Early in his reign, King Solomon went to Gibeon to offer sacrifices at a sanctuary that predated the building of the temple in

Jerusalem. During this time of worship, the Lord invited Solomon to ask for anything he might desire. Here at Gibeon, Solomon asked for and received the wisdom for which he is remembered (1 Kings 3:4–15).

Bethel is another city in Benjamin with a long history of biblical significance. Bethel is located approximately 12 miles north of Jerusalem on the ridgeline that served as the road for the patriarchs moving north and south in the Promised Land. After Jacob had deceived his father, Isaac, and taken the blessing away from his brother, Esau, his life was in danger. Rebekah, his mother, urged him to flee and live in Haran until his brother's anger had cooled. Jacob began a trip north on the Ridge Road (Patriarch's Highway) and arrived at Bethel. Here he had a dream in which he saw a ladder or stairway leading into the sky and the angels of God ascending and descending on it. The Lord Himself was standing at the top assuring Jacob that the promises He had extended to Abraham and Isaac were still in place, and that divine presence and protection would accompany him on his travels. When Jacob awakened, he gave this place the Hebrew name "Bethel," which means "the house of God" (Genesis 28:10–19). Bethel lived up to this name at a later date in Israel's history. Apparently the ark of the covenant resided in Bethel for a time before its transfer to Shiloh (Judges 20:18).

But darker days were ahead for Bethel. After the kingdom of Solomon divided, King Jeroboam I ruled the northern portion of that kingdom. He was deeply concerned that his subjects living in the northern portion of the Promised Land would travel to Jerusalem to worship there. Jerusalem was part of the Southern Kingdom ruled by David's son Rehoboam. He was afraid that if his people did that regularly, they would agitate for a reunification of the kingdom with David's son as their king. So he appointed priests and initiated festivals to rival those in Jerusalem. He commissioned the creation of two golden calves and built worship facilities within his own kingdom to house them. The cities he chose were Bethel and Dan. The selection of Bethel is strategic given the road systems. It meant that anyone in his Northern Kingdom who was traveling south to Jerusalem on the Ridge Road (Patriarch's Highway) would have to travel right past his more convenient sanctuary in Bethel on the way (1 Kings 12:28–30).

7

JUDAH AND THE JUDEAN WILDERNESS

The promise that God made to Adam and Eve in the Garden of Eden was fulfilled many centuries later in the small village of Bethlehem. Here, in a shelter designed for animals, the designer of the world and the author of our salvation was born. We traditionally celebrate Jesus' birth on December 25, but is that the time of year Jesus was actually born? And what can we know about the appearance of the animal shelter that served as His birthplace? Many of us picture a nativity scene with a wooden barn, but is that how the birthplace of Jesus actually looked? By examining subtle, geographical clues in Luke 2, we will find direction in answering those questions.

This, of course, will mean a trip to the region of the Promised Land called Judah. More significant biblical history is associated with this region than any other in Israel. Here among the barren mountain heights is where we find Bethlehem, the home of King David and the birthplace of Jesus. Here we find the Judean Wilderness, a refuge for David as he fled from the jealous spear of Saul and a proving ground for Jesus where He faced the temptations of Satan. But most importantly, this is where we find Jerusalem, a city captured by David, made beautiful by Solomon, and made magnificent in the death and resurrection of Jesus.

A map will quickly show that Judah lies in the heart of the central mountain zone. But it takes a walk through this region to be impressed by its rugged, mountainous topography. Following the lead offered by changes in geology and rainfall, we will divide Judah into an eastern and western section. First, we will examine the western portion of Judah, the Judean Highlands. Second, we will turn our attention to the eastern portion of this region, a place so void of rainfall that we will call it the Judean Wilderness.

THE JUDEAN HIGHLANDS

Boundaries and Dimensions

From the air, the Judean Highlands stand out as an oval cluster of higher mountains stretching some 40 miles between Benjamin in the north and the Negev in the south. The width of this region varies between 10 and 15 miles. On the eastern side, a narrow moat separates the Judean Highlands from the Judean Wilderness. A similar moat on the western side separates it from the foothills called the Shephelah. The residents of the Judean Highlands knew a high degree of security. The rugged mountain ridges and narrow V-shaped valleys make the Judean Highlands both inaccessible and very defensible. But the residents of Judah sought to enhance their security by controlling the natural buffer zones found immediately to the east, west, and south of the Judean Highlands. To the east lies the Judean Wilderness, to the south lies the Negev, and to the west lies the Judean Shephelah.

Topography and Geology

The mountains of the Judean Highlands rise quickly and dramatically from the foothills that lie immediately to their west. Subsurface pressure surged from beneath and forced the terrain upward into massive waves of stone (a geological upfold).[1] Among those random waves, a continuous ridge formed through the center of Judah. This central ridge extends from Jerusalem to Hebron reaching elevations over 3,200 feet above sea level before rolling out into the dry foothills of the Negev. From Hebron, this single ridge breaks into two distinct ridges that descend in the direction of Arad and Beersheba. These two ridges are the natural roadways leading into the interior of the hill country.[2]

Standing on those mountains, you may look in any direction and see more and more of the same thing, bare rocks and loose stones washed free of soil.[3] The deforestation that began when Joshua and the Israelites entered the land continued through the centuries that followed. Once the root systems of the native trees were no longer in place to prevent the soil from washing away, as much as 3 feet of topsoil eroded from the hillsides. Over 60 percent of the Judean Highlands have eroded down to the underlying Cenomanian limestone. Apart from bare rocks and loose stones, the other surface characteristic that attracts our attention is the terraces. Almost every hillside is covered with terraces that have formed naturally and that have been enhanced through centuries of farming. These terraces become even more important in this region due to the very narrow V-shaped valleys that carve their way between the mountains. The base of these valleys are often only 20 yards or so in width leaving very little room for crops to be grown. (See photo 12.)

Natural Resources

The Cenomanian limestone harvested from these mountains becomes an important natural resource for builders in the ancient world. Cenomanian limestone contains significant concentrations of silica and calcium. This results in a very durable stone that erodes at a rate of 1 centimeter every thousand years.[4] If you had enough money to quarry this durable stone, you could construct buildings that lasted for centuries. Thus the foundations of structures that were built by King Solomon nearly 3,000 years ago have survived for visitors to see today.

This Cenomanian limestone erodes into the moisture-absorbing terra rossa soil we have discussed above. Where this soil combines with more significant rainfall along the ridge between Bethlehem and Hebron (20 to 28 inches annually), rich crops and produce may be grown. (See photo 13.) Recall that the Israelites who had spent months in the desert were very impressed by the produce that the exploration party brought back from Hebron (Numbers 13:23–24). However, not every location in the Judean Highlands is blessed with the same amount of water. Rainfall is distributed unevenly here with the northern portion of the region receiving more precipitation than the southern portion. Rainfall also diminishes from west to east creating both a wet and dry slope to the mountains.

As in all of Israel, the residents of Judah were deeply concerned about procuring sufficient water. But the families living here were particularly concerned because the springs alone would not provide sufficient water for the daily needs of a family. That is why the residents in the hill country dug openings in the earth's surface called cisterns. These water collection systems were cut into the earth's surface and plastered to make them watertight. They were designed to capture the seasonal rains and hold them for use throughout the dry season. Such water systems typically did not replace the need to get fresh water from a well or spring, but they did reduce dependence on other water sources.

Culture

The Judean Highlands have often been called the stronghold of the country because residents there enjoyed a very high degree of security from outside invasion.[5] The hills of Judah are clearly off the beaten path. George Smith quips that while "Galilee is on the road to everywhere, Judah is on the road to no where."[6] In fact, no major road penetrates the interior of this region, so Judah is cut off from direct contact with the international trading routes. This is bad news for both the merchant and the advancing army. The high mountains and narrow valleys made the Judean Highlands a very undesirable military target. Too much time would be spent and too many lives would be lost in an assault on this citadel. Given that the economic value of this region is not high enough to offer a significant return on this investment, invaders of this land will typically pass on the Judean Highlands and focus instead on the more easily conquered and more lucrative coastal plain. The only exception to this rule is when the empires feel a need to make a point by destroying the capital city, Jerusalem. But even when Jerusalem becomes the target of such a conquest, the attack is usually delayed until the surrounding territory has come under fire. The leaders of the empires hope that such isolation would cause Jerusalem to surrender before a lengthy and expensive siege is begun.

Those who enjoy this high degree of security pay for it with land that is less amenable to agriculture. Ridges that have little topsoil and valleys with very narrow floors force farmers to terrace the hillsides in a bid to develop sufficient surface area for planting. Over 56 percent of the Judean Highlands are covered by humanly enhanced terraces.[7] These terraces both increase the surface area that may be farmed, capture the eroding soil, and slow the runoff rate after a rainfall so that the precious moisture may be absorbed by the soil.

Such terraces involve a significant amount of thought and effort. It is estimated that one acre of terraced land would require the investment of four to twelve years worth of labor.[8] A blocking wall must be built out of stone that will enhance the steps that form naturally in these mountains. The material placed behind that wall must be carefully chosen and arranged to allow for just the right amount of drainage while leaving an adequate bed of soil for the roots. This construction process creates a shelf that is anywhere from 50 to 100 feet in width. And the job is not finished after the terrace is built. The terrace walls need constant maintenance from year to year. If the blocking wall is damaged in any way, the hydraulic pressure from the next rain would begin to undo all the hard work that had been put into the construction of this agricultural environment.

By contrast to Samaria in the north, the farmers in Judah were more likely to produce grapes than olives. These grapevines in the hill country, like those that Jesus spoke about in John 15, are typically not grown on trellises where the dry wind would quickly rob the plant of its moisture. Rather, the grapes are trained to grow just a few inches off the ground, with a rock placed beneath the vine to hold it high enough so that the ripening fruit will not touch the ground. (See photo 29.) Because the grapes ripen at the close of the dry summer season, they rely heavily on dew to supply their water needs. By contrast to many farm fields in the United States, rocks are left in and around the agricultural fields where the grapes are being grown. These rocks increase the surface area on which dew can collect and provide even more of this unique summer moisture to the plant. The farmers also address the threat of evaporation by growing the grapevines closer to the ground. The shade from the grapevine's foliage retards the rate of evaporation from the soil and from those rocks left around the base of the plant where the moisture is collecting. Once harvested, the grapes would be used both for food and for making wine. Depressions were cut into the bedrock where the farmer and his family could step on the grapes and extract the juice. This juice was taken from the winepress to a cool place where it might ferment into wine. Given the shortage of water and contamination of water sources, wine was commonly consumed as a beverage in Israel.[9]

Pastoralism also flourishes in the hills of Judah. Families during the time of the Bible would typically shepherd a herd mixed with goats and sheep. Both are important to the diet and daily needs of the residents. Sheep provided wool, meat, and hides for various applications. Goats provided the same but are distinguished by their milk production. The ancient family would get its milk supply from the goat rather than the sheep because the goat produced twice the quantity of this important beverage.[10] Thus the typical Israelite family would have both sheep and goats and would shepherd them together in a group. Sheep that are left in a herd by themselves threaten the ground cover by their constant grazing.[11] By contrast, the goats move regularly as they eat. Because the sheep follow the goats, they are kept on the move to eliminate the overgrazing that increases erosion.[12] Eventually those mixed herds are again separated, giving Jesus the metaphor of the sheep and goats which He used to describe the final judgment (Matthew 25:31–33).

Biblical History

Several locations in the Judean Highlands will draw the attention of the careful Bible reader. We begin with Hebron. Hebron is located 19 miles south of Jerusalem on the central ridgeline of this region. The higher elevation of the mountains here (3,343 feet) pushes the rainfall totals to an average of 28 inches per year. The open basins that have formed around Hebron and the significant rainfall create a very fertile environment with copious wells, springs, and agricultural fields. The exploration party sent out by Moses from Kadesh Barnea in order to visit and report on the Promised Land brought back produce from this region to show the Israelites the agricultural potential of the Promised Land (Numbers 13:22–24).

Various roads radiate out from this key city to En Gedi on the Dead Sea, to Beersheba and Arad in the south, to Beth Guvrin in the west, and to Bethlehem and Jerusalem in the north. As these roads radiate to places that favor the production of different commodities, Hebron becomes the ideal meeting point for those wishing to trade pastoral or agricultural commodities. Bedouin from the south would bring sheep, donkeys, and cattle to trade for produce like grain, olives, grapes, pomegranates, and other fruit from the hill country.[13] Hebron also had a very important theological role to play in the Old Testament. God had promised Abraham that his family would inherit this land and become the nation that would bring the Messiah to the world. It was here at this busy hub of local commerce that Abraham built an altar commemorating that promise (Genesis 13:18). When his wife, Sarah, died, Abraham bought a plot of land here that had a cave on it called Machpelah (Genesis 23:9). This was the first portion of the Promised Land that Abraham actually came to own personally. It served as a critical down payment and testimony to the hope that Abraham's family would own this land and bring the Messiah to the world. In time, Abraham, Isaac and Rebekah, Jacob and Leah would join Sarah in this cave tomb (Genesis 25:9 and Genesis 49:29–32). Eventually, Herod the Great built a structure over the area where the cave was traditionally located that today is called the Haram el-Khalil ("The Friend of God," see 2 Chronicles 20:7). Due to the high regard accorded the Patriarchs both in the Christian, Jewish, and Muslim faiths, the structure remains to this day and is divided into both a synagogue and mosque. After the time of the Patriarchs, King David also placed his mark on this city. Following the death of Saul, David was able to put the southern portion of Israel under his control. Hebron became the capital of this kingdom as David worked to put the rest of Saul's former kingdom under his control as well (1 Kings 2:11).

Of course, no trip through Judah would be complete without a stop in the city of Bethlehem. Micah had promised that it would be the birthplace of Jesus (Micah 5:2) and, in time, that is what it became. Bethlehem is located just 5 miles to the south of Jerusalem. Here the narrow, V-shaped valleys of the Judean Highlands widen into open basins filled with rich soils. These fields favor the abundant grain crops that undoubtedly helped shape this village's name. Bethlehem is the Hebrew equivalent of "House of Bread." On the hillsides above those valleys lie many threshing floors. Once the grain was harvested in the fields, the mixture of chaff and seed were carried to these threshing floors for threshing and winnowing. Animals would be walked across the harvested crop, sometimes pulling a threshing sled. (See photo 13.) The hooves of the animal and the stones embedded in the sled would break the bond between the seed and the husk. When the Mediterranean sea breeze began later in the day, the farmer would throw the mixture of grain and chaff into the air with a winnowing fork. The heavier grain would fall back to the threshing floor while the lighter chaff would be blown downwind. As the chaff contained the seeds of many weeds, that mixture was then burned to prevent their return to the fields.[14] It was on such a threshing floor that Ruth presented herself to Boaz at harvest time (Ruth 3). The activities on the threshing floor also provided John the Baptist with the language he used to describe

Judgment Day. "His winnowing fork is in his hand, and he will clear his threshing floor, gathering his wheat into his barn and burning up the chaff with unquenchable fire" (Matthew 3:12).

After the harvest, many of the local herdsmen and farmers would enter into contracts that permitted the shepherds to bring their flocks into the agricultural fields. The animals would pick through the harvested field for any leftovers that they might find, while at the same time leaving behind manure that would fertilize the soil in advance of the next planting season.[15] David was a shepherd who grew up in Bethlehem (1 Samuel 16:1–13). He may have tended flocks that were participating in such a contract. That certainly appears to have been the case with a group of shepherds who happened to be working the night that Jesus was born. Angels appeared to announce the birth of Jesus to shepherds who were tending their flocks in those fields (Luke 2:8). Here is a subtle but persuasive clue about the time of Jesus' birth. Because shepherds were not allowed into the agricultural fields until after the harvest, and as the harvest was not completed until the end of June, the most likely time for Jesus' birth would be sometime in July or August.

Geography also offers us a clue about the animal shelter in which Jesus was born. Families in the Bethlehem area took advantage of the naturally forming limestone caves and employed them as shelters for their animals. (See photo 14.) Some of these shelters were adjacent to the living quarters, but sometimes the cave itself became the basement of the home. Such a cave plays a key role in understanding the details of Jesus' birth. After Mary and Joseph traveled to Bethlehem for the census, they would likely have approached the home of one of their relatives living in Bethlehem. When they did so, they were told that the guest room (κατάλυμα) was already in use. Note that this guest room (often mistranslated as "inn") is not a roadside inn that rented rooms to travelers. Such a commercial place of lodging did exist, but it is called a πανδοχεῖον. Luke uses this word later in his Gospel account to describe the inn to which the Good Samaritan took the injured man (Luke 10:34). Mary and Joseph asked for permission to use the guest room. This guest room was not available for them, but they then were offered the cave in which the animals were kept. It is not clear whether this cave was the basement of the home or adjacent to it, but it definitely was not a wooden barn. Wood was plentiful enough in Europe for the construction of such a shelter for animals, but construction grade lumber was so scarce in the Promised Land that it was primarily reserved for the construction of roof rafters. That is, unless one had the wealth of Solomon with which to important cedar from Lebanon. Wood was typically not used in framing the walls of a home and certainly would not have been used for building a barn for animals. All the cultural indicators suggest that the most likely place of Jesus' birth was a cave.

Today the traditional site of Jesus' birth, the Church of the Nativity, is built over such a cave. Christians as early as Justin Martyr (*Dialogue* 78, ca. AD 100) were able to point to the cave where this birth had traditionally taken place. When Emperor Hadrian wished to eliminate the Christian heritage associated with this cave (AD 135), he erected a pagan worship site dedicated to Thammuz (Adonis). He apparently hoped to destroy the memory of Christ's birthplace. But by marking the spot with a pagan worship site, he inadvertently prepared the site for rediscovery and rededication to the Christian memory at the time of Emperor Constantine.[16] The mother of this Christian emperor built a church here in AD 339 to commemorate the birth of Jesus and teach theology to those who would travel to this sacred spot. Although this church structure was severely damaged following the Samaritan uprising, Emperor Justinian rebuilt it on an even larger scale after AD 529. This structure was spared from total destruction again during the Persian invasion (AD 614) when many other Christian churches were destroyed. The Persian soldiers are said to have spared the church due to a mosaic on the facade of the church depicting the Magi in Persian dress. Substantial portions of this Justinian church still survive in the Church of the Nativity, which may be visited today.

Christians visiting the Promised Land may also wish to commemorate another important event in Jesus' life with a visit to Bethany. The village of Bethany was located just 1.5 miles from Jerusalem and was the home of Mary, Martha, and Lazarus. This family extended hospitality and lodging to Jesus and the disciples when they were in the area of Jerusalem (Luke 10:38). This invitation must have been particularly welcome during the festivals in Jerusalem when the city itself was teaming with pilgrims and the demand for lodging more than doubled the price of an overnight stay. The friendship that developed between Jesus and this family certainly deepened the sadness He felt when news arrived that Lazarus had died. This set the stage for one of the most dramatic miracles recorded by the Gospel writers. When Jesus arrived in Bethany, Lazarus had already been in the tomb for four days. Nevertheless, Jesus lifted the hope of this family with words that have touched the hearts of grieving families for centuries. "I am the resurrection and the life. He who believes in Me will live, even though he dies; and whoever lives and believes in Me will never die" (John 11:25–26). Jesus then proceeded to the tomb and showed His power over death by calling Lazarus back to life. As early as the fourth century AD, a Byzantine church was built near the traditional location of this miracle with access to the tomb itself. Portions of the floor from this early church may be seen in the courtyard of the current Church of St. Lazarus. The tomb itself, visited by Christians for centuries, may also be entered today. This great miracle of Jesus restored Lazarus to his grieving family, but at the same time it pushed the Jewish leadership to agitate for Jesus' death (John 11:45–50). As Jesus was eating His last meal in Bethany with this reunited family on the Saturday before Palm Sunday, the Jewish leadership was planning not only His death but also the death of Lazarus because news of the resurrection was bringing many more followers to Jesus (John 12:10–11).

Of course, the most profound moments in the history of this world are associated with Jerusalem. This city is located on the border between the tribal territory of Benjamin and Judah. Here we focus briefly on the geography of Jerusalem.[17] The ancient city of Jerusalem resides at 2,500 feet above sea level and rests on five separate mountains that are bisected by three major valleys. The Kidron Valley lies to the east separating the Temple Mount from the Mount of Olives. The Hinnom Valley defines the southern and western extent of the city, while the Central Valley (also called the Tyropoeon Valley, that is, the Cheesemakers Valley) extends from the Damascus Gate in the north to the Hinnom Valley in the south. A map may be helpful in understanding the layout of ancient Jerusalem, but an extended walk about the confines of biblical Jerusalem will provide the best lesson in the topography of the city. Nearly every step taken in this city will be followed by a subsequent step up or down. And should you choose to walk from one end of the city to the other, you will experience several hundred feet of elevation change climbing and descending between valleys and hills.

This city that is built on five hills is also surrounded by hills that are even higher, a fact alluded to in Psalm 125:2. Here the inspired writer emphasizes the permanence of God's presence with His people by comparing it to the enduring presence of the mountains around Jerusalem. "As the mountains surround Jerusalem, so the LORD surrounds His people both now and forevermore" (Psalm 125:2).

The austerity of natural resources makes Jerusalem an unusual candidate for an important city. Typically, significant cities reside on accessible seashores or along navigable rivers. They are sometimes located along an overland trade route or are blessed by considerable natural resources.[18] Jerusalem has lots and lots of rocks scattered about its hillsides, but enjoys none of those qualities we often associate with a capital city. What is more, the available water is less than that which would be necessary to sustain a large city. Two springs served the ancient population, the En Rogel Spring and the Gihon Spring, both located in the Kidron Valley. The Gihon Spring flows at a rate that is more than ten times that of the average spring in the region, but was capable of providing water for only about 120,000 people.[19] Consequently, when Herod the Great expanded the city, he was forced to build an aqueduct system that carried water in from the hills lying south of Jerusalem to supply water for the growing population. Given the paucity of natural resources, it is no wonder that the ancient geographer Strabo observed, "Jerusalem is not a place looked on with envy nor yet one for which anyone would make a serious fight."[20]

What did make the city desirable was its natural defenses. Jerusalem was in the heart of the Judean Highlands. As we have seen, that alone would make it difficult to attack. But the hill and valley system on which Jerusalem was built made it a citadel difficult to storm and conquer. Before the time of King David, the Jebusites held this piece of land calling it Jebus. They mocked David and his army, using less than politically correct language, saying that even those who were physically and visually challenged would be able to defend their city against an assault by David (2 Samuel 5:8). But David did go on to capture the hill on which the Jebusite city sat. From this point on, that hill with the 12-acre summit becomes Mount Zion, the city of David.

After the time of David, Solomon increased the size of the city from 12 to 32 acres by including the hill immediately to the north of the city of David. On that northern hill is where Solomon constructed his royal palace and the temple itself (1 Kings 6–7). Later, in the days of King Hezekiah, another significant expansion of the city occurred. The threat of an Assyrian invasion, and with it the hundreds of refugees that would flee to Jerusalem, led King Hezekiah to increase the walled portion of the city to 125 acres and include an underground water tunnel that would bring a regular flow of fresh water from the Gihon Spring to the Siloam pool (2 Chronicles 32:30). The Jerusalem in which Jesus walked had expanded to 450 acres and been carefully adorned by the hand of Herod the Great. His passion for grandiose architecture is clearly evident both in the enhancements around the temple and in the other public buildings throughout New Testament Jerusalem. If Jerusalem had a weakness topographically, it is that it lies to the north. That is undoubtedly why Herod strengthened the fortress protecting the north wall of the city, calling it the Antonia Fortress.

We cannot leave this city without brief mention of the most important event in history associated with Good Friday and Easter Sunday. The exact location of Jesus' crucifixion and resurrection are debated. But the earliest evidence would suggest that the current Church of the Holy Sepulcher is built over New Testament Calvary. This spot had been a stone quarry but was retired due to micro fractures in the stone. By the time of the first century it had become a garden and cemetery, subsequently used for the execution of Jesus. An alternative site for Calvary is the quiet garden called Gordon's Calvary, named after the British general, Charles Gordon, who popularized the location in 1883. A visit to Gordon's Calvary will afford the visitor a more realistic sense of what that setting would have looked like. However, a trip to the Church of the Holy Sepulcher places us near the spot of our greatest victory.

THE JUDEAN WILDERNESS

Boundaries and Dimensions

Immediately to the east of the Judean Highlands we find the forbidding, mountainous wasteland of the Judean Wilderness. This geographical region lies between the high mountains of Judah and the desiccated shores of the Dead Sea. It is approximately 60 miles in length by 10 miles in width, stretching from the Wadi Auja (5 miles north of Jericho) to the Wilderness of Zin.[21]

Topography and Geology

While the mountain ridges and deeply cut, V-shaped valleys of the Judean Wilderness recall the topography of the Judean Highlands, here the terrain takes on an even more rugged and menacing appearance. (See photo 17.) Barry Beitzel captures the image well when he says, "This is a genuine desert: it is a solitary, howling, rough and rocky wasteland that is nearly devoid of plants and animals and virtually without rainfall."[22] From the air, we may trace approximately 20 narrow, parallel gorges through the region, each aligning itself on an east-west axis perpendicular to the Dead Sea. From the ground, the impression we get of this wilderness will depend on our point of entry. Traveling from the Judean Highlands into the Judean Wilderness, we are not as struck by a change in topography as we are by the increasing dryness of the slopes we pass. But traveling from the Dead Sea into the Judean Wilderness, we are most struck by the ruggedness of the terrain. The Judean Wilderness climbs dramatically from the shore of the Dead Sea in a series of steps. The first of these steps is the most dramatic, for it consists of a near vertical ridge that rises between 300 and 1,200 feet before the eyes of westbound travelers. If those travelers continue to the west, they will meet a subsequent series of ridges climbing in oxygen-depleting steps. A trip from the edge of the Dead Sea to the central ridge of the Judean Highlands will mean a climb from 1,300 feet below sea level to over 3,000 feet above sea level in just a little over 10 miles.

Geologically, the region presents a fairly consistent structure that is most apparent in those places where the steep ridges have eroded to reveal the geologic cross section. The lower layers of the Judean Wilderness are composed of harder limestone and dolomite with softer chalk layers above.[23] When caught in the right light, these layered escarpments offer some of the most beautiful scenery in the Holy Land.

Natural Resources

But such beauty does little to quench the thirst that builds in the low humidity of this wilderness. If water is a precious commodity in the Promised Land, it is doubly so here. Over half of this region receives less than 8 inches of annual precipitation.[24] And that total diminishes to just 2 inches at the southern end of the Dead Sea. The position of the Judean Wilderness on the east side of the rising terrain in Judah accounts for this meager amount of rainfall. Moist air is forced upslope on the west side of the mountains,where it cools and gradually loses its moisture. When that same air mass crosses the mountains and begins to descend into the Jordan rift valley, it again begins to warm. As the dew point of that descending air rises, the rain and clouds disappear, leaving the land east of the mountains in a sunny, rainfall shadow. That means two cities as close together as Jerusalem and Jericho can have dramatically different climates. Although these two cities are less than 15 miles apart, Jerusalem receives 22 inches of annual precipitation while Jericho receives 5 inches.

The problems caused by this scarcity of rain are compounded by the surface geology in this wilderness. The water that falls from the sky does very little to benefit life here because the composition and slope of the surface resist the absorption of this rain. Thus the little rain that falls runs off quickly. As it collects in the canyons, its volume and velocity can increase dramatically. The flash floods that were a real threat to the ancient travelers moving up the narrow gorges of the Judean Wilderness can also threaten and inconvenience the modern traveler. The author has been held up more than once on the shores of the Dead Sea, when the violent waters of a flash flood raged out of the Judean Wilderness threatening to sweep cars and buses from the road into the Dead Sea.

The apparent wealth of water that rages through the canyons during a flash flood stands in contrast to the lack of springs that exist within the Judean Wilderness itself. These springs are a product of the unique geologic structure lying beneath the surface. On the surface, there is a watershed line marking the highest elevations on the mountain ridges. As most of the rain falls to the west of that line, the majority of water begins its journey west toward the Mediterranean Sea. But underground, a tilt in the layers allows some of the water that falls to the west of the topographic watershed line to actually travel east beneath the surface and break out as springs in the wilderness.[25] It is springs like those of Ein Qilt, Ein Feshkha, and En Gedi that made it possible for humans to remain in the wilderness for any extended period of time.

The extreme conditions of this wilderness make it difficult for animal and plant communities to survive without special adaptation. For example, the gazelle is capable of going for weeks without water by relying upon the moisture it derives from the plants that it eats.[26] Of course, the gazelle counts on the fact that certain plants will survive in this wilderness.

The plants that do must develop strategies that allow them to survive in such a rigorous climate. Some produce leaves only during the wetter months of the year, then lose them and transfer the function of the leaves to the stem during the dry time. Some produce deep root systems that seek water from well below the earth's surface. Other plants produce wide and shallow root systems designed to capture the moisture left in the soil by the dew. Still others may produce very high osmotic pressure that literally vacuums moisture from the soil around them.[27] Because larger plants would require more water, trees of moderate size are absent in this harsh environment except for the occasional acacia tree.

Culture

Given the lack of rainfall and poor soil conditions, the farmer did not find a home in this rough and rugged region. Bedouin herding their sheep and goats will penetrate the edges of the region, but only when the winter rains suggest some greenery on the northern slopes where evaporation is less pronounced. Agricultural life and shepherding were not part of the culture in the Judean Wilderness.

The geography here did not favor the traveler either. Typically, regions with Senonian chalk on the surface are areas that make for good travel arteries boasting valleys that are boulder free and dry quickly.[28] But it is not so much the geology as the topography and hydrology of the Judean Wilderness that creates problems for the traveler. Travel north and south through the region is prohibitive because it was blocked by a series of near-vertical ridges that run east and west. Those who are traveling east and west must contend with the lack of water and rugged terrain. For example, entering the region from the Dead Sea basin required a significant climb. Smith described the 500 foot climb above En Gedi "not so much a pass as a staircase."[29] The gorges offered a tempting alternative to such climbs, but they are generally too narrow and dangerous for transportation. This means the travelers would be forced up on the steep sides of the mountains where the trails would move along precarious pathways strewn with foot-damaging flint and where one misstep could spell disaster. The threat of dehydration was also very real. This trip across the Judean Wilderness would typically take between five and eight hours.[30] And the amount of exertion required to make that trip was significant. The summer heat and low humidity of the desert conspired to dehydrate all who would dare walk its pathways. Thus it was imperative to carry sufficient water to cover the entire time of the trip and to use that water in a very judicious way.

Travelers who made the journey attempted to pass through this region in the minimum amount of time. But there were individuals who chose to live in the Judean Wilderness. Because this wilderness was a place that most members of society avoided, it served as "a refuge for rebels, fugitives and hermits."[31] As such, it was a land to get away from the rigors, limitations, and threats of society itself. This function of the Judean Wilderness was particularly apparent during the Byzantine period. At this time, over 60 monasteries clung to the sides of the Wadi Qilt and Nahal Kidron, housing those who wished to escape the ease of a more settled life for the ascetic life found in this wilderness.[32]

Soldiers would also have been billeted in this wilderness because the Judean Wilderness served as the eastern buffer zone for those living in the Judean Highlands. Any invasion coming from Moab, Edom, or the Arabian Desert would first pass through this region.[33] Because this invasion route would need to begin at a water source, the location of lookout posts may be found at places like Jericho and En Gedi where freshwater springs were found. These lookout posts were not designed so much to repulse an invasion as they were to send an early warning to those living in the mountains that trouble was on the way (2 Chronicles 20:2).

Biblical History

When David fell into disfavor with King Saul, he fled to the Judean Wilderness emerging only briefly before retreating there again and again (1 Samuel 22–27). The water from the spring at En Gedi provided David with welcome relief while the caves in the area provided shelter. It was here, near the spring of En Gedi, that King Saul used a cave as we might use a restroom. As fate would have it, David and his men were hiding in that very same place. Although Saul was completely vulnerable and David's men urged him to seize this moment to dispatch his rival, David only cut off a corner of Saul's robe in respect for the Lord's anointed king (1 Samuel 24:1–7). David's time in the Judean Wilderness also provided him with language and images for his psalms. The psalm superscription says that David wrote Psalm 63 while he was in this wilderness. He speaks about his longing for God as having the same intensity as his thirst in this desert. "O God, You are my God, earnestly I seek You; my soul thirsts for You, my body longs for You, in a dry and weary land where there is no water" (Psalm 63:1).

The Judean Wilderness was also home to the beginning of John the Baptist's ministry. The austerity of the environment was in many ways a perfect backdrop for his message: "Repent, for the kingdom of heaven is near" (Matthew 3:2). And by preaching in the wilderness, John fulfilled the prophecy that Isaiah had made concerning the Messiah's forerunner, "A voice of one calling in the desert, 'Prepare the way for the LORD, make straight paths for Him'" (Matthew 3:3).

Jesus also visited the Judean Wilderness. As He began His earthly ministry, Jesus was led here by the Spirit to face the temptations of Satan. After forty days of isolation and fasting, Satan came to Him with His first temptation to turn the plentiful stones in the region into the absent bread. He refused this temptation, citing the greater importance of God's Word for nourishment (Matthew 4:1–4).

One more place deserves mention even though no biblical event is clearly linked to it. Masada is a butte on the far eastern side of the Judean Wilderness overlooking the Dead Sea. The sheer, 600-foot walls rise over 1,300 feet above its surroundings. The first evidence of its fortification is linked to Alexander Jannaeus (103–76 BC) who used it to protect his southeastern border. But it was Herod the Great who turned it into the 50-acre fortress that towers over the Dead Sea to this day.[34] Visitors will see the remains of palaces, storehouses, baths, swimming pools, and cisterns (able to hold 1.5 million cubic feet of water). But the site is preserved today not because of Herod the Great, but because it is a symbol of Jewish resistance to oppression. After the Romans destroyed Jerusalem in AD 70, 967 Jewish men, women, and children seized this stronghold and held out here against the Romans. Roman general Flavius Silva began a three-year siege of the fortress, building a wall and eight fortified camps around Masada to prevent food and water from reaching those on the summit. At the end of three years, when it became apparent that the Romans would soon enter the fort, those within struck an agreement with one another. They would take one another's lives rather than allow the Romans to come in and kill them. Of the 967, only two women and five children escaped by hiding in a cistern. They are the ones who lived to tell the story.[35]

THE JUDEAN SHEPHELAH AND NEGEV

The Judean Shephelah and the Negev share an important connection with the Judean Highlands. They are the foothills that lie immediately to the west and south of the Judean mountains, respectively. Because these regions contain the access routes leading to the interior of Judah, they function as buffer zones used to control access to the hill country. While they have a common geographical function, the Shephelah and Negev present a very different geographical picture. Because the foothills of the Shephelah lie to the west, they receive a considerable amount of rain. Hence, they are the wet foothills. The Negev lies further to the south and away from rising terrain. This means that the Negev region houses the dry foothills.

Like the Judean Highlands to the north, the Shephelah and the Negev serve as the stage for significant biblical events. We will see that the Negev provided the home base for the patriarchs, while the Shephelah valleys witnessed the escapades of Samson as well as the victory of David over Goliath. Once the children of Israel had taken possession of these regions during the days of Joshua, they fought again and again to maintain their right to live there. It was just such a fight between the Israelites and Philistines that brought about the duel between David and Goliath. Of all the details of that story that are familiar to the average Bible reader, the details about geography have often gone unnoticed. As the biblical author established the stage for that contest, he carefully defined the setting for the reader. "Now the Philistines gathered their forces for war and assembled at Socoh in Judah. They pitched camp at Ephes Dammim, between Socoh and Azekah. Saul and the Israelites assembled and camped in the Valley of Elah" (1 Samuel 17:1–2). The careful placing of this battlefield has a significant impact on the way we view the character of King Saul and David. In order to deepen our appreciation of that language, we will turn our attention to the Judean Shephelah.

JUDEAN SHEPHELAH

Boundaries and Dimensions

The Judean Shephelah extends approximately 30 miles from the Aijalon Valley in the north to the Lachish Valley in the south. This region is slightly wedge-shaped widening from 6 miles in the north to 10 miles in the south. Five distinct east-west valleys travel though this region. From north to south, they are the Aijalon Valley, the Sorek Valley, the Elah Valley, the Guvrin Valley, and the Lachish Valley. The western ends of these valleys spill out into the coastal plain. The eastern end terminates in a north-south chalk valley (Wadi Ghurab and Wadi Sar) that lies between the Shephelah and the rising terrain of the Judean mountains.

Topography and Geology

The Hebrew name for this region, Shephelah, is derived from a Hebrew word that calls attention to the humble or low elevation of the hills found here. By contrast to the mountains of Judah that lie immediately to the east, the rising terrain of the Shephelah is much more humble in size and appearance. Topographically, the region is composed of hills (300–1200 feet above sea level) that rise to less than half the height of the mountains in Judah.[1] These hills form ridges that generally align themselves on an east-west axis. (See photo 15.) A core sample from these hills reveals that they have a soft limestone core and are covered by a 3- to 5-foot crust that is called nari.[2] Between those parallel ridges we find valleys that open toward the Mediterranean Sea. By contrast to the mountains to their east where harder limestone has formed narrow V-shaped valleys, the softer Eocene limestone has eroded into broad, U-shaped valleys filled with fertile, alluvial soils.[3]

Natural Resources

The higher terrain that lies immediately to the east of the Shephelah guarantees this region as much as 20 inches of precipitation. As the moist air masses are forced upslope and cooled, the life-giving water is released on the hills and valleys below. This not only means an adequate supply of water for ripening grain crops but also plentiful groundwater that may be tapped via springs or wells.

The Shephelah was also a prime source for chalk. Industrial mining of this chalk is particularly apparent when visiting the Bell Caves in the Guvrin Valley where over 800 caves are found. Miners worked aggressively here from the sixth through the tenth centuries AD harvesting the chalk for use as mortar and plaster. They would begin by cutting a circular opening through the hard nari that was approximately 1 meter in diameter. The miners would then excavate downward up to 80 feet in ever widening circles, then bring up 15-pound blocks of chalk that could be more easily handled and transported. This procedure left behind very distinctive caves that have a bell-like shape.[4] Today, a national park preserves the right of visitors to explore these bell caves.

The sycamore tree was another natural resource harvested in the region (1 Kings 10:27; 1 Chronicles 27:28).[5] This tree produced lumber that was used in roof construction of ancient buildings. The fruit from the sycamore is called a fig. It is harvested in the fall as a food product, though it is considered inferior in taste when compared to the true fig due to its lower sugar content. Consequently, this less desirable fig carried a lower selling price and was typically consumed by the poor.[6] In order for it to ripen properly, the young, green fruit had to be pierced and wiped with oil at the end of summer. At this time of year, shepherds could be seen sitting in the trees dressing figs to make some additional money as they kept watch over their sheep in the valley floor.[7] Amos makes reference to this work when his detractors criticized his message of judgment against the Northern Kingdom and the sanctuary at Bethel. In his own defense, he asserts that he was an ordinary man who had been called to higher service. "I was neither a prophet nor a prophet's son, but I was a shepherd, and I also took care of sycamore-fig trees. But the LORD took me from tending the flock and said to me, 'Go, prophesy to my people Israel' " (Amos 7:14–15).

It was not only the fig but also the wood from the sycamore tree that made the Shephelah ridges economically valuable. Because the porous structure of the wood kept the weight of the limb to a minimum, while at the same time providing the limb with considerable strength, it was used as roof beams in the construction of homes and public buildings.[8] The persistence and regenerative powers of this tree made it possible to manipulate the tree into producing even more timber than it would naturally. If a single limb is cut from the tree, it will restore itself by producing multiple limbs at the same spot. If a windstorm removes the soil from the roots, the root system will expand to compensate. If the soil is blown over the tree and covers it, the sycamore will grow roots from its former branches and send new shoots above the ground.[9] As an ancient form of timber management, forestry practice dictated that a mature sycamore tree must be cut down. From the stump that is left behind, numerous limbs would grow that are ready for harvest and use as roof beams within six years.[10]

Culture

Those living in the Shephelah would take advantage of the topography and natural resources in different ways. The wide and fertile valleys that receive ample rainfall and have good drainage are ideal places for growing grain and grapes. These same crops would not grow on the hard nari of the hills lining those valleys. But this is exactly where the sycamore tree flourishes, providing both figs and lumber to the landowner. The gentle slope and east-west orientation of these valleys also means that they are well suited for transportation. This is particularly true of the broad Aijalon Valley that, to the casual observer, resembles a plain much more than a valley.[11] As such valleys are the natural transportation routes, they are thought of as roads. It is the difference between a wide-open valley and the narrow V-shaped valley that may provide the imagery for Jesus' statement: "Enter through the narrow gate. For wide is the gate and broad is the road that leads to destruction, and many enter through it. But small is the gate and narrow the road that leads to life, and only a few find it" (Matthew 7:13–14).

Each of the five Shephelah valleys provide access to the interior of Judah in much the same way; valleys lead to ridges that lead to key cities of the interior. For example, the Aijalon Valley leads to the Beth Horon Ridge that eventually leads to Gibeon and Jerusalem. The Sorek Valley meets a ridgeline that climbs steadily to Kiriath Jearim and, via the Rephaim Valley, to Jerualem. In the same way, the Elah Valley leads to Bethlehem and the Guvrin and Lachish valleys lead to Hebron. Thus, key cities and forts were built along these access routes to control entry, making the Shephelah the western buffer zone for those living in the Judean Highlands.[12] The Shephelah valleys are also military thoroughfares whose control will determine the fate of those living in the secure shadows of the Judean Highlands.[13] That is what makes a city like Gezer such a critical location. Gezer lies at the far western end of the Aijalon Valley where it meets the coastal plain and the International Highway. Anyone wishing to live with a measure of security in Jerusalem will only find that security when friendly forces hold Gezer.

Biblical History

Given the value of this region, it is no surprise that the Shephelah valleys make more than a few appearances on the pages of our Bible. During the time of Joshua's invasion of the Promised Land, five Amorite kings attempted to block the march of Joshua down the Benjamin plateau by attacking Gibeon. The army of Israel marched all night from Gilgal mounting a counter attack the next morning. As the attack began, the Lord threw the Amorites into a confused retreat before Joshua and his soldiers. The Lord then guaranteed the final outcome by providing a great miracle. The summer months in Israel are absolutely dry, and it is during the dry season when kings go to war. Then there is no rainfall to impede their travels, and even clouds are absent from the sky. But this day, the Lord provided both comforting clouds as protection from the sun's rays[14] and a hailstorm that killed hundreds of enemy fighters retreating through the Aijalon Valley (Joshua 10:1–15).

Many of the exploits of Samson are closely connected to the Sorek Valley. He was born in the small village of Zorah on the hills above Beth Shemesh. During his lifetime, the Israelites were dueling for control of this valley with the Philistines. Samson was the judge who would carry on the fight and relieve Israel from the Philistine oppression. He married a Philistine girl whose hometown was Timnah on the west side of the Sorek Valley (Judges 14). But when the wedding celebration went sour and his new wife was given to another man, Samson's rage brought havoc to the Philistine economy when he burned their wheat fields in the Sorek Valley just as the harvest was about to begin (Judges 15:1–5).

The duel between the Philistines and Israelites for the Shephelah valleys continued into the time of the last judge, Samuel. When the Israelites were experiencing defeat at the hands of the Philistines, they determined that it would be helpful to bring the ark of the covenant to the frontline of the battle. In doing so, they seem to be taking a page from the playbook of the Canaanites. The Canaanites had practiced sympathetic magic. They believed that through various incantations or actions that they were able to force their deities to do what they wanted. Apparently, this way of thinking had also infected the Israelite leadership. Using the ark of the covenant as a talisman, they attempted to manipulate divine favor and victory in their battle with the Philistines. Of course, God is not so small as to be manipulated by such a ploy, so he allowed the ark to be captured by the Philistines (1 Samuel 4). On the other hand, the Lord was not about to let the Philistines think that they controlled him. So everywhere the ark went among the Philistine cities, it brought trouble with it (1 Samuel 5). Finally, they sent it back to the Israelites on a new cart being pulled by two cows that had recently calved. Those cows walked away from their calves directly down the Sorek Valley toward Beth Shemesh where the ark of the covenant again returned to the Israelites (1 Samuel 6:12).

But that is not the last we hear of the Philistines. In 1 Samuel 17, the Elah Valley serves as the stage for the battle between David and Goliath. The inspired author locates the geographical setting of this story very precisely. "Now the Philistines gathered their forces for war and assembled at Socoh in Judah. They pitched camp at Ephes Dammim, between Socoh and Azekah. Saul and the Israelites assembled and camped in the Valley of Elah" (1 Samuel 17:1–2). This allows the geographically informed reader to superimpose this battle on the terrain very easily and employ that geography in the interpretation of these events. On the one hand, the location of this battle signals the importance of this conflict. When we consider the value of the agricultural land being contested and the critical nature of this valley as a buffer zone for Saul's kingdom, the importance of this military conflict becomes clear. The Philistines had penetrated deeply into the Elah Valley setting up camp between Socoh and Azekah. This intrusion was of monumental significance. But if the geography articulates the national crisis facing Israel, it also participates in showing just how unfit

Saul has become as a leader. The people had made it clear that their king must be someone who would, in their words, "go out before us and fight our battles" (1 Samuel 8:20). Here at a moment of significant national crisis, we are unimpressed with the leadership of Saul because both he and his men were discouraged and terrified in the face of Goliath (1 Samuel 17:11). But the geography does more than show the importance of this battle for the nation; it also shows that this military incursion into the Elah Valley had personal ramifications for David. David's home was in Bethlehem just a little more than 15 miles from Azekah. If the Philistine army would continue east down the Elah Valley following the most natural route up the Husan ridge, they would arrive in Bethlehem in less than one day. Of course, David goes on to defeat Goliath and turn the Philistine incursion into a Philistine retreat. In the process, he removes a significant national threat to the nation while proving himself to be every bit the man of God who is fit to rule in Israel. The Shephelah may not have a very striking appearance on a map, but stories such as these show the critical importance of this small region to the history and well-being of ancient Israel.

NEGEV

Immediately to the south of the Judean Highlands lie the dry foothills known as the biblical Negev. The Hebrew word *negev* is used to indicate the cardinal compass point of south. In the minds of the Old Testament authors, the Negev represented the southern extent of Israel's holdings. They speak of the traditional boundaries of the Promised Land by using the expression "from Dan to Beersheba," Beersheba being one of the major cities of the Negev. In Hebrew, *negev* also carries with it the connotation of dryness.[15] As one moves farther south in the Promised Land, the amount of precipitation diminishes and forms a link between that cardinal compass point and dry terrain. Its name tells us something about the location and quality of the land we find here.

Boundaries and Dimensions

The modern state of Israel has designated a region called the Negev that is somewhat larger than the Negev of the Old Testament. The modern Negev extends from the city of Beersheba south through the Paran Plateau and the Eilat Hills before touching the shores of the Gulf of Eilat.[16] This is considerably larger than the Negev of the Bible whose boundary lines are somewhat harder to define. The authors of the Old Testament describe the Negev as starting around the city of Beersheba and extending south to Kadesh Barnea (Genesis 20:1; Numbers 13:21–22). The western border of this region begins where the sand dunes on the Mediterranean Sea end and the eastern border terminates on the ridge that runs above the Arabah.

Topography and Geology

Topographically, the Negev is composed of low, round hills that are cut by shallow gullies and ravines of varying size. In the northern portion of the biblical Negev, a larger basin has formed that houses the urban centers of Beersheba and Arad. (See photo 18.) This basin rises gradually from 150 feet near the sea to 800 feet at Beersheba and is surrounded by rising terrain on all sides.[17] A larger wadi system consisting of the Nahal Beersheba and the Nahal Besor drains this basin in the direction of the Mediterranean Sea.[18]

The Negev is covered by a fine, yellow-brown soil that is easily carried by the winds (loess soil). A core sample of this region reveals that this soil reaches a depth of over 100 feet near Beersheba.[19] The fine, almost powdery soil resembles the stone-free surface of a desert. At first glance, this soil would appear to have limited value as an agricultural field. But this loose soil is very fertile and will produce very viable grain crops when sufficient water is present.[20] However, the presence of water creates another complication in farming this land. When it rains, the grains of this soil swell and coalesce into a hard crust allowing for only a small amount of moisture to penetrate below the surface. The water runs off quickly and tears open gullies that zigzag back and forth, which ultimately create the topographic relief described above.[21]

Natural Resources

As the name Negev or "dry" suggests, there is less rain and less predictable precipitation in this region. The farm fields here receive between 8 and 12 inches of rain.[22] But when the winter rains fall, the surface structure that resists water penetration shunts most of the rainfall into the larger wadi systems. As these wadis are riverbeds that flow with water for brief periods of time and then quickly dry out, the water-filled wadi is used as a metaphor by the psalmist in a prayer appealing for success. "Restore our fortunes, O LORD, like streams in the Negev" (Psalm 126:4). But as quickly as this water begins to flow, it ceases. The residents of the Negev are forced to pursue their water needs by digging wells in the wadis themselves where the water table is closer to the surface.

The two trees that are most common in the Negev region are the white broom acacia and the tamarisk. Both make a unique contribution to the lifestyle of those living or traveling in the region. The white broom acacia is a medium-sized bush that is wider at the top and narrower at the bottom. Even though the profile of this tree offers very little protection from the sun, it is a welcome sight to the traveler moving through a nearly treeless landscape where even a small amount of shade is considered precious. Given the uniqueness of this tree in the region, it is likely the bush used by Hagar to shelter Ishmael when she was fleeing from the household of Abraham (Genesis 21:14–15). By contrast, in the cooler winter months a warm and long-lasting fire may be produced by the acacia tree when the dry branches of this tree are placed into a campfire.[23] When Elijah was fleeing from Ahab, he found shelter under such an acacia and was nourished by food cooked over its glowing embers (1 Kings 19:3–6).

The other tree that we find in the Negev is the tamarisk. This tree is capable of withstanding both the heat and the long dry spells in the Negev because it has a deep root system to tap into the subsurface moisture. When Abraham was in the vicinity of Beersheba, he planted a tamarisk tree near a well that he had obtained (Genesis 21:33). In this treeless region, his plan was to produce a shady spot for those who would find rest at the side of this well. But his selection of this type of tree was no accident. Not only is the tamarisk well suited to the conditions of the Negev, it also provides a form of natural air conditioning to those who sit beneath it. During the night, when water from the atmosphere condenses on cooler collecting surfaces, droplets form on the leaves. More water than usual collects on the tamarisk because the leaves themselves produce tiny salt crystals. The next day as the atmosphere warms and the water droplets begin to evaporate, the area around the tree itself cools and creates an inviting micro-atmosphere beneath the tree.[24] Abraham chose wisely when he selected the tamarisk to be placed next to the well.

Culture

Life in the Negev has never been easy. The combination of loess soil and meager rains meant that a successful barley crop was only possible every three to four years.[25] Thus the ordinary residents of the Negev tended not to be farmers but pastoralists like the patriarchs who spent the more moist months of the year in the Negev, but moved north with their flocks during the dryer summer months.

More permanent settlement in the Negev was possible, but those residents were dependent upon a strong and interested central government that was able to resist the attacks of the Bedouin from the desert and aid the local population when threatened by the inevitable drought.[26] Such a government grew attentive to this more austere land because it held a unique position on the trade routes and functioned as the southern buffer zone for the Judean Highlands. Trade goods moving from Petra in the mountains of Edom to Gaza on the Mediterranean Sea would move through the Beersheba basin. In addition, the Way to Shur that connected the Judean Highlands with Egypt also passed through Beersheba. That placed Beersheba at a north-south, east-west crossroads, uniquely positioned to service travelers and tax their goods. Of course, the same road system that carried merchandise also expedited the footsteps of invading armies. Thus, the Negev functioned as the southern gate through which an invader from the south could penetrate the country.[27] Whenever there was a strong central government ruling in the Judean Highlands, they would use the Negev as a military buffer zone staffed and guarded by soldiers living on this frontier.

Biblical History

The biblical events most associated with the Negev are closely connected to the cities of Beersheba and Arad. Today, one may visit a carefully kept, 3-acre site that preserves archaeological evidence of the way Beersheba would have looked at the time of Samuel. Although there is no archaeological evidence of a city existing at the time of the patriarchs, it is their story that is most closely linked with the Negev and Beersheba. In fact, the name Beersheba (Hebrew for "well of the seven" or "well of the oath") is linked to events in the life of Abraham and Isaac (Genesis 21:25–31 and 26:28–33). As the patriarchs and their families were Bedouin people who moved regularly with their animals, it is best to think of these families living in the Negev for a period of time during their seasonal migration. A clearer understanding of this landscape will help us read the stories related to herding animals, digging wells, and fighting for water rights with greater appreciation. After the time of the patriarchs, the Bible reader meets Beersheba as a regional, administrative center whose streets are walked by military commanders, tax collectors, priests, and merchants.

Beersheba, which resides 45 miles southwest of Jerusalem, becomes the reference point for the southernmost extent of the Promised Land in the phrase, "from Dan to Beersheba" (Judges 20:1, 1 Samuel 3:20, et al). When Jacob was leaving the drought-stricken Land of Israel for Egypt, he paused here at Beersheba. He hesitated before setting foot outside of the Promised Land even though this action threatened reunion with his son Joseph. So the Lord Himself appeared to Jacob in a vision and assured him that his temporary departure from this land had divine sanction (Genesis 46:1–7). Sometime later, Beersheba served as an administrative and military complex controlling the southern border of the country. When Samuel's age prevented him from leading Israel effectively, he appointed his two sons, Joel and Abijah, as judges. Their corruption became evident within the city gate of Beersheba where they lived (1 Samuel 8:1–3), precipitating the request that Samuel appoint a king to lead the nation.

The city of Arad also presents itself in an impressive way to the contemporary visitor. It lies approximately 16 miles to the east of Beersheba. Here an Early Bronze, walled city that dates to the time before Abraham sprawls over 25 acres of land. This city was a Canaanite commercial center associated with the lucrative trade route that connected Gaza with the King's Highway. Long after this city ceased to exist, an Israelite fort (unmentioned in the Old Testament but likely built during the time of Solomon) still stands as a sentinel watching for hostile activity to the south and southeast. Within that 150- x 150-foot Israelite fortress with 12-foot thick walls, we find a sanctuary complex that roughly mimics the complex prescribed for the temple in Jerusalem. This complex has an altar that matches the size and construction technique demanded by God (Exodus 20:25 and 27:1) as well as a room that has been called the "Holy of Holies." Since the temple at Jerusalem has been destroyed, this is the only enduring example of an Israelite sanctuary discovered to date. It may have been constructed to support the worship needs of the soldiers on duty at Arad and subsequently destroyed during the religious reforms of

King Hezekiah or Josiah. The biblical authors also mention a Canaanite king who lived in the Negev. The King of Arad resisted the initial invasion of the Israelites into the Promised Land (Numbers 21:1–3), but was eventually defeated by Joshua (Joshua 12:14). The archaeological evidence at the current site of Arad does not indicate the presence of a city at the time of Moses and Joshua. This suggests that either the current excavation of Arad is incomplete, that the Arad of Moses' and Joshua's day is best associated with a different location in the Negev, or that Arad is being used as a regional designation rather than as an urban designation.

9

MOUNT HERMON, HULEH BASIN, AND THE SEA OF GALILEE

Our geographical explorations have taken us through the first two zones of the Promised Land. We have explored the sea, harbors, and fields of the coastal plain. We have explored the hills and strongholds of the central mountain zone. Our journey through the Promised Land will now set foot in the rift valley. This part of Israel clearly shows its membership in the 4,000-mile long Afro-Arabian rift valley that begins in Turkey and extends to the great lakes of Africa.[1] This intrusion into the earth's surface causes elevations within the Jordan rift valley to plunge hundreds of feet below sea level. We will soon see how this physical reality impacts both the climate and culture of this extended valley.

Our look at the rift valley will actually begin on the tundra of Mount Hermon. The snow-capped peaks may seem like an unusual place for us to begin looking at a valley that is mostly below sea level, but this mountain makes a significant contribution to geographical realities that await us. From the tundra we will venture south through the Upper Jordan River, the Sea of Galilee, the Lower Jordan River, and the Dead Sea. You will soon realize that we are exploring the most diverse zone of the Promised Land. We will encounter tundra snowfields, sub-alpine forests, palm-laden jungles, and trackless deserts. This chapter will focus upon the northernmost portions of the rift valley visiting Mount Hermon, the Huleh Basin, and the Sea of Galilee.

This northern segment of the rift valley is that portion of Israel where Jesus spent the great majority of His earthly ministry. Cities like Korazin, Bethsaida, and Capernaum saw more miracles than any other cities in the Promised Land. Yet this apparent blessing actually led to a condemnation of those cities that had the greatest opportunity to participate in this ministry of Jesus.

> Woe to you, Korazin! Woe to you, Bethsaida! If the miracles that were performed in you had been performed in Tyre and Sidon, they would have repented long ago in sackcloth and ashes. But I tell you, it will be more bearable for Tyre and Sidon on the day of judgment than for you. And you, Capernaum, will you be lifted up to the skies? No, you will go down to the depths. If the miracles that were performed in you had been performed in Sodom, it would have remained to this day. (Matthew 11:20–23)

Let us now turn to this portion of the Promised Land so that we may more clearly see what the residents of those cities did not see.

Mount Hermon

Location and Dimensions

Mount Hermon is the southernmost peak of the Anti-Lebanon Mountains, whose base lies approximately 25 miles north of the Sea of Galilee. In reality, Mount Hermon is not an isolated peak but a cluster of peaks that dominate the northern horizon rising to an elevation of 9,262 feet above sea level. The biblical authors also refer to this mountain with the Phoenician name, Sirion, and the Amorite name, Senir (Deuteronomy 3:9). On a clear day, the snow-capped peaks may be seen from many locations in the Jordan rift valley. Thus for residents of the biblical world, it was what they considered the highest mountain (Psalm 42:6). Today, the massive Mount Hermon resides as a border between three countries: Lebanon, Israel, and Syria. It served a similar role in the Bible denoting the northernmost extent of the Promised Land (Deuteronomy 3:9 and Joshua 11:17).

Natural Resources

Mount Hermon is best known for its two natural resources: water and cedar. In a land where water is so very scarce, Mount Hermon stands out as a dramatic exception to the rule. It receives over 60 inches of annual precipitation.[2] A portion of that precipitation is held in permanent snowfields on the tundra, but the majority of that water percolates through the limestone core to form abundant springs whose waters combine to form the Upper Jordan River. (See photo 22.) Thus mention of Mount Hermon and abundant water are closely linked. When Jeremiah expressed horror at the notion that the nation of Israel could forget about their God, he said that it would be more likely for Mount Hermon to run out of water than for this people to forget their Lord. "Does the snow of Lebanon ever vanish from its rocky slopes? Do its cool waters from distant sources ever cease to flow? Yet my people have forgotten me . . . . " (Jeremiah 18:14–15).

But Mount Hermon is also a critical source for construction-grade lumber. The cedars of Lebanon grow up to 98 feet tall with bases up to 6.5 feet in diameter.[3] Construction-grade lumber is also very scarce, so the cedar harvested from Mount Hermon is very valuable. Its attractive red tones, its enticing aroma, and its resistance to rot make it the most costly and prestigious lumber for construction.[4] That is why David contracted with Hiram, King of Tyre, for lumber to build his palace (2 Samuel 5:11). Solomon also contracted with Tyre for lumber used in constructing the temple (1 Kings 5:6) and his own palace. The use of cedar in Solomon's palace was so breathtaking that it was called "The Palace of the Forest of Lebanon" (1 Kings 7:1–5).

Culture

Given its location and size, Mount Hermon forms a block that funnels traffic on the International Highway past its lower flanks. Thus this mountain and the cities at its base have a more international flavor to them. During the first days of Jesus' earthly ministry, Satan attempted to derail His mission of salvation by tempting Jesus to sin. In the third of those temptations, "the devil took Him to a very high mountain and showed Him all the kingdoms of the world and their splendor" (Matthew 4:8). While Mount Hermon is not specifically named in this biblical text, the description fits this geographical location better than any other in Israel.

While standing on this mountain, the ancient observer could see representatives of the entire world pass by.

As the enormity of Mount Hermon combined with other geographical realities effectively narrows the travel options, cities at the base of Mount Hermon play a key role in controlling access to the Promised Land from the north. Two cities, Dan and Caesarea Philippi, were located at the base of Mount Hermon and served as the guardians to this northern gate during the biblical period.

Biblical History

The dominant city at the base of Mount Hermon during the Old Testament period was the city of Dan (also called Leshem in Joshua 19:47 or Laish in Judges 18:7). The tribe of Dan had been assigned a portion of land near the Mediterranean Sea but the Danites were unable to hold that portion of the Philistine Plain. They eventually moved north and took over the city of Laish, renaming it Dan. Subsequently, this city becomes the northern boundary of the Promised Land and is used repeatedly by the biblical authors to describe the extent of the Promised Land, "from Dan to Beersheba" (for example, Judges 20:1). The area around the ancient city is a thickly-forested nature preserve that recalls the way the area would have looked in the biblical period.[5] Those forests are fed by a significant number of springs that percolate from the base of Mount Hermon and form the headwaters of the Upper Jordan River. The springs in the area produce 250 million cubic meters of water each year,[6] spawning whitewater rapids, icy pools, and beautiful waterfalls.

Among the archaeological ruins in Dan, the visitor may see a Middle Bronze gate that is 50 feet wide and 20 feet high. This gate dates to the time of Abraham and may have been used by him during his rescue of Lot (Genesis 14:14). But it was Jeroboam I who put Dan on the map in a more infamous way. After the rule of Solomon, his kingdom was split into a northern section (still called Israel) and a southern section called Judah. Jeroboam I was the first king of the new "Israel" and he was concerned about people going south to Judah for worship at the Temple in Jerusalem. He assumed that such a trip would kindle a desire for reunification of the Davidic kingdom, so he built worship sites at Bethel and Dan placing a golden calf in each (1 Kings 12:25–33). He then said to his subjects, "It is too much for you to go up to Jerusalem. Here are your gods, O

Israel, who brought you up out of Egypt" (1 Kings 12:28). The sacred area within the city of Dan has been excavated and the platform or "high place" at which the gold calf was worshiped is preserved to this day. Geography dictates that this city would also be an important military and administrative center as the northern gate to Israel. A massive gate structure and segments of the defensive wall dating back to Ahab and Omri also remind us of this role the city played as an administrative post and fortress.

Caesarea Philippi lies just 2 miles east of Dan on the southwest flank of Mount Hermon. Like Dan in the Old Testament, Caesarea Philippi in the New Testament had cultic, military, and administrative functions. Herod the Great built a white marble temple here and dedicated it to Emperor Augustus. After the death of Augustus, his son Philip received this city. He is the one who named it Caesarea. And in order to distinguish it from the port city on the Mediterranean Sea, it became known as Caesarea Philippi.[7] As visitors enter Caesarea Philippi today, they are met by the intimidating glare of a large, ominous cave yawning at the base of the mountain (45 feet high and 65 feet wide). During the first century AD, water poured from this large cave and under the temple built by Herod, and created a very otherworldly scene. The appearance of the cave was so awe inspiring that during the Hellenistic and Roman periods it was proclaimed to be the entrance to hades, the passage to the underworld.

Jesus took His disciples to this region in order to have a more sustained discussion about His identity. The setting for this discussion is striking. First, note that Jesus speaks with the disciples about His divine identity and mission against the backdrop of this pagan worship site that is a symbol of Roman power and influence in the region. Jesus asks His followers who they believe Him to be. Peter offers the answer, "You are the Christ, the Son of the living God" (Matthew 16:16). Jesus not only accepts this identification as the Messiah but celebrates its meaning. Here at the base of the massive rock, Mount Hermon, and near the cave that is viewed as the gate of hades, Jesus proclaims, "And I tell you that you are Peter, and on this rock I will build my church, and the gates of Hades will not overcome it" (Matthew 16:18). Here, as He did so often, Jesus uses the geographical setting of this conversation to add clarity and power to His teaching.

HULEH BASIN

Location and Dimensions

Below Mount Hermon, we happen upon a lake nestled in the middle of a bowl with rising terrain on all sides. The lake in the valley is called Lake Huleh (also spelled Hulah; Josephus calls it Lake Semechonitis) and the valley is called the Huleh Basin. The basin extends southward toward the Sea of Galilee for approximately 16 miles and stretches 5 miles from east to west. There is a slight fall in the elevation of this valley as you move from north to south, but that change is difficult to perceive. Thus, the basin has the appearance of a sprawling, flat valley.

Natural Resources

Water is again the defining element of this region. The Huleh Basin receives between 16 and 25 inches of annual precipitation.[8] However, it is not the direct rainfall but the runoff from Mount Hermon that contributes the bulk of water to this ecosystem. The Huleh basin receives approximately 740 cubic meters of water each year from the snowmelt and springs of Hermon.[9] Because the basin lies 230 feet below sea level, and thousands of feet below the snowfields of the 9,262-foot Mount Hermon, it serves as a natural sump for the area. But once the water arrives in this basin, it cannot leave easily because it is blocked by a basaltic dam that formed naturally on the south side of the valley. The water that collects in this basin may leave through the narrow gorge cut through that basaltic plug or seep down through the soil; but in either case, this is a slow process. That means that the Huleh Basin of biblical times was an impenetrable, papyrus marsh.[10]

Culture

This marsh provided an ideal habitat for various forms of wildlife. During his visit to the region, William Thomson noted the presence of panthers, leopards, bears, wolves, jackals, hyenas, fox, gazelle, and wild boars.[11] And given the ideal habitat for migrating birds, this basin became a critical estuary along their migration route.[12] But what was great for the animals was not ideal for humans. The Jewish settlers who moved into this region in the 1920s and 1930s contracted malaria on a regular basis. That and the need for more agricultural land led the modern state of Israel to drain the

Huleh Basin in the late 1950s. In doing so, more than 30,000 acres of agricultural land with dark, alluvial soils became available for cultivation.[13] But this also meant that the waters entering the Sea of Galilee were no longer naturally filtered through this marsh. This decision continues to have a negative impact on the turbidity and ecological well-being of the Sea of Galilee.[14]

Biblical History

One city from the biblical record deserves mention here; that is the city of Hazor. It lies approximately 10 miles north of the Sea of Galilee on the hills that rise above the west side of the Huleh Basin. Geography determined that this should be an important city as it guards a key north-south, east-west crossroads. The north-south component of that crossroads is formed by the International Highway. It is forced up onto the hills along the western side of the Huleh Basin to avoid the perils associated with the lowland marsh. One segment of this road travels to Hazor, then northwest to Tyre and north to Baalbek before turning east across the Fertile Crescent. Thus Hazor stands as an important fort and administrative center along this major north-south artery. But geographical realities have also created an east-west road in the vicinity. Of course, Lake Huleh would have blocked east-west traffic across the basin. Farther to the south, another natural roadblock prevented easy east-west movement. There, the Upper Jordan River plunges into a gorge that cuts through the basaltic dam and reaches for the Sea of Galilee. This gorge is over 1,200 feet deep[15] with rushing water that drops 680 feet in less than 9 miles.[16] It constitutes a barrier to east-west travel that is just as effective as the lake itself. But between Lake Huleh and this gorge was a place where the Upper Jordan River could be forded. That spot is marked today by the Bridge of Jacob's Daughters. At precisely this spot, just south of Hazor, travelers on the International Highway would turn northeast toward Damascus.

At a spot where fertile soil, rich agricultural fields, and an international crossroads come together, one would expect an important city to grow, and we are not disappointed. During the time of Joshua and Judges, Hazor was a massive Canaanite city. From the eighteenth to the thirteenth centuries BC, Hazor covered more than 200 acres, which made it the largest city in the region.[17] Joshua captured and burned this city because it allowed the northern coalition of kings resisting the Israelite entry into the land (Joshua 11:10–11, 13). The city shows up again in Judges 4, when the Lord uses Jabin, the King of Hazor, to oppress the Israelites during a time of spiritual carelessness. When the Israelites call to the Lord for help, he uses Deborah and Barak to defeat this powerful city-state (Judges 4 and 5). The critical location of Hazor was not lost on the Israelites. When Solomon became king, he fortified the city so that he could extract trade revenue from the merchants and resist invasion from the north (1 Kings 9:15).

SEA OF GALILEE

The water from Mount Hermon that drains through the Huleh Basin eventually finds its way into a large, freshwater lake. In the Old Testament, the name of that lake was the Sea of Kinnereth (Numbers 34:11 and Joshua 12:3).[18] In the New Testament, this lake goes by several names: the Lake of Gennesaret (Luke 5:1), the Sea of Tiberias (John 6:1; 21:1), and the Sea of Galilee (Matthew 4:18 and Mark 1:16).

Location and Dimensions

The lake itself is somewhat oval in shape but with a deeper protrusion into the western shoreline. (See photo 25.) Given the amount of New Testament history connected to this lake, it is a favorite stop for Christian pilgrims. But most modern visitors find it to be much smaller than they had assumed it to be. The Sea of Galilee is approximately 13 miles long and 8 miles wide, making the opposing shorelines clearly visible from either side. It has a circumference of just 32 miles and a depth of 180 feet.

The lake and its shoreline reside within a large basin approximately 700 feet below sea level. With the exception of the southern shore, it is surrounded by terrain that rises 1,280 feet above the shoreline. (See photo 24.) Cities such as the Decapolis city of Susita (Hippos) were established on the hills that rise above the seashore. Susita was founded on the eastern side of the Sea of Galilee as a Roman city whose mission was to control the steep ascent on the Roman road from Beth Shan to Damascus.[19] During the night, the lights of this city would be clearly evident to those on the west side of the lake. Jesus may well have had this city's lights in mind when He spoke of the Christian life in Matthew 5: "You are the light of the world. A city on a hill cannot be hidden" (Matthew 5:14).

Prominent plains between the shoreline and the mountains present themselves on the northwest and northeast shores of the lake. The plain on the northwest shore is called the Plain of Magdala or the Plain of Gennesaret. The plain on the northeast side of the lake is called the Plain of Bethsaida.

Geology

The water and geology of this basin show a clear relationship to the volcanic and seismic activity of the rift valley. While the water that enters the Sea of Galilee from the Huleh Basin is fresh, the water within the lake itself is comparatively saline due to the warm salt water springs that dot the shoreline and percolate up from the lake bed.[20] At Tabgha (Heptapagon), seven hot springs enter the lake. These hot mineral baths, often seen in places like Tiberias, soothe muscles and begin the process of salinization in the lake water that reaches its ultimate conclusion in the Dead Sea.

The geology of the lake region is also indicative of the earlier volcanism in the region. The predominant surface stone around the lake is not limestone, but basalt. This black basalt stone is particularly evident in the ancient structures built in cities like Capernaum and Korazin. The soils found on plains around the lake have a darker appearance. They are excellent for farming because they are comprised of limestone, chalk, basalt, and organic matter.[21] To put that in perspective, the farm fields on the Plain of Gennesaret alone were capable of providing 16,000 people with the grain they would need for an entire year.

Culture

The Sea of Galilee provided those who lived on the shoreline with a variety of business opportunities including agriculture, dying and tanning, international trade, fishing, boat building, and fish curing.[22] The International Highway that connects Africa with Asia and Europe skirts the northwest shore of the Sea of Galilee near cities like Capernaum.[23] Businesses that supported this trade would have grown up along the lakeshore including those hired by the Romans to exact a tax on the merchants using that highway. Apparently Matthew was in charge of such a tax-collection station near Capernaum when Jesus called him to become one of His followers (Matthew 9:9).

The rich plains, adequate rainfall, and mild climate of the basin created an ideal environment for the farmer to grow both grain and fruit crops.[24] And even the stones provided the residents around the Sea of Galilee with a unique business opportunity. Certain practical and industrial applications required that stone be used in a high friction environment. Stone door sockets, steps, thresholds, door lintels, drainpipes, channels, grinding stones for grain, and olive pressing stones are examples of such applications.[25] As basalt is more durable than limestone, the basalt boulders from the Sea of Galilee were harvested and manufactured into such furnishings and tools.[26]

The fishing industry also took pride of place in the Sea of Galilee basin. Sixteen harbors that supported this industry have been identified along the lakeshore. Typically, such a harbor would have had a breakwater, pier, promenade, repair shop, administrative buildings, storehouses, and a tax station.[27] Once fish were harvested from the lake they needed to be processed, so stations were set up at cities like Magdala (Taricheae). The ancient geographer Strabo observed that fish caught in the Sea of Galilee were of excellent quality and apparently even had found their way to the markets in Rome.[28] Given the predominant nature of this occupation along the lake and Jesus' regular presence on its shores, we find Jesus' ministry and teaching making contact with this enterprise. Recall that Peter, James, and John were summoned from their occupation as fishermen to become His apostles and that fishing is mentioned more than just a few times in His teachings.

But there was more than one way to fish the Sea of Galilee, and those different fishing techniques show up in the biblical record. At times, reference is made to the dragnet. The dragnet was a long net, 750 to 1,000 feet in length and up to 24 feet in height. The top rope of the net was fitted with floats and the bottom of the net was fitted with stone weights. This kind of net was used for fishing near the shoreline. A boat would take one end of the net about 100 yards from shore while men held the other end on the shore. This wall of netting would then be walked and pulled along the shallows of the lake perpendicular to the shore until the boat swung in to the shore corralling the fish in the shallows where they would be harvested.[29] This type of net is mentioned in Ezekiel 47:10 and Habakkuk 1:15. Jesus also used the image of the dragnet in a parable when speaking of Judgment Day. "Once again, the kingdom of heaven is like a net that was let down into the lake and caught all kinds of fish. When it was full, the fisherman pulled it up on the shore. Then they sat down and collected the good fish in baskets, but threw the bad away" (Matthew 13:47–48).

A second type of net used in fishing the Sea of Galilee is the cast net. The cast net is a circular net that is 20–25 feet in diameter with weights attached all around the perimeter of the net. This kind of net was also used in the shallow waters near the shoreline. The fisherman would swing this net overhead to open it up to its full diameter. It would then be cast on the water where it would sink and trap the fish beneath it.[30] Apparently, Simon and Peter were using a net like this when Jesus called them. "As Jesus walked beside the Sea of Galilee, he saw Simon and his brother Andrew casting a net into the lake, for they were fishermen" (Mark 1:16).

A third method of fishing seen in the Gospels employs a trammel net to fish in the deeper water of the lake. The trammel net was a compound net with three layers. Like the dragnet, the top rope of the net had floats and the bottom rope of the net had stone weights attached to it. The outer and inner walls of the net were tied into 5- x 5-inch squares through which a fish could easily pass. The innermost layer was of a much finer mesh (less than 2 inches square) through which the fish could not pass. The goal was to panic the fish so that they would rush into the net and become entangled between the two layers. This type of net was used to fish in the deeper waters of the lake at night when the fish couldn't see as well. A boat was used to encircle an area. After the net had been put into place, the fishermen would move into the center of the net-like coral, make noise to scare the fish, and the fish would then flee into the unseen net from which they were gathered.[31] This type of fishing is being practiced in Luke 5:1–11 and John 21 where Jesus provides a miraculous catch during the daylight rather than the night hours.

Biblical History

The Sea of Galilee was also the stage for miracles of Jesus involving the wind (Mark 4:35–41 and John 6:16–21). In the first instance, Jesus and the disciples were using a boat to travel during the evening hours to the east side of the Sea of Galilee. They were caught in a fierce windstorm that threatened their very lives. At first, it may seem strange that this group of men with experienced, local fishermen aboard would get caught in such a storm. But the wind that created this furious squall was the sharquia wind. The sharquia is a wind that develops locally and unexpectedly due to the unique geography of the lake basin. A temperature inversion can occur on cool evenings leaving a warm air pocket in the Sea of Galilee basin. As the heat from the hills above radiates away, colder air can rush down the 1,300-foot mountains around the lake with such force that it churns the lake violently and creates 6-foot waves in a matter of moments. It is likely this unexpected sharquia wind was the wind that threatened the boat in Mark 4 and set the stage for Jesus' miraculous calming that left the disciples asking, "Who is this? Even the wind and the waves obey Him!" (Mark 4:41).

The northwest side of the Sea of Galilee enjoyed a very wealthy and prosperous community. The international trade, agriculture, basalt industry, and fishing industry made it possible for one to become extremely wealthy. But wealth has the ability to distort priorities. People who benefited so dramatically from the natural resources God provided in the basin could easily lose sight of the God who had made their wealth possible. Because Jesus taught frequently on the shores of the lake, He had the opportunity to address mistaken thinking about wealth on a number of occasions. For example, the parable of the rich fool (Luke 12:13–21) presented in this wealthy arena showed that even rich people may be impoverished if they are not rich in what God has to offer.

Of course, Jesus spoke about a great many more things to His hearers on the shores of Galilee. A significant part of Jesus' earthly ministry occurred within a triangle formed by connecting the cities of Capernaum, Korazin, and Bethsaida, the so-called evangelical triangle. The Gospel writers make it clear that Jesus did more miracles within this triangle than in any other location (Matthew 11:20–25). What we know about these cities varies greatly. The Gospel writers' only mention of Korazin is in Jesus' denunciation of this city. Bethsaida was the home of Philip, Andrew, and Peter (John 1:44) and the area most likely used by Jesus for the feeding of the 5,000 (John 6:1–15).

But Capernaum is clearly the most important city. We have a considerable amount of information about Jesus' ministry here. We read in the Gospels that He preached and healed in this city on a regular basis (Matthew 8:1–17 and 17:24–27; Mark 1:21–34 and 2:1–12; Luke 7:1–10; John 4:46–54, et al). Matthew explains that Jesus left His hometown of Nazareth and established a base of operations in Capernaum in fulfillment of Isaiah's prophecy (see Isaiah 9:1–2). "Land of Zebulun and land of Naphtali, the way to the sea, along the Jordan, Galilee of the Gentiles—the people living in darkness have seen a great light; on those living in the land of the shadow of death a light has dawned" (Matthew 4:15–16). The darkness of the basalt stone that covers this region is illustrative of the spiritual darkness that so permeated this region.

The residents of this area needed a message of hope and salvation, but so did the rest of the world. And in this respect, the location of Jesus' ministry in Capernaum is also clearly related to geography. Even though the city of Capernaum only had a population of about 1,200 people, it had international potential.[32] The message that Jesus offered was meant for the entire world. Consequently, Jesus could either travel the world to deliver His message of hope to each continent, or He could position His earthly ministry where representatives of each continent would encounter the message during their travels. Capernaum lies near the International Highway. This crossroads between Asia, Africa, and Europe carried not only the commodities of international trade but also news and information. By establishing a base of ministry in this critical location, Jesus could be assured that word of His message and miracles would find its way into the rest of the world even before the miracle of Pentecost.[33] In these days following the expansion of Jesus' ministry to the ends of the earth, it is ironic that travelers from all over the world still come to Capernaum in order to see the foundations of the synagogue where Jesus spoke, and the home of Peter that served as his headquarters. (See photo 27.)

Herod Antipas also left his mark on the west shore of this lake. This son of Herod the Great built Tiberias during the days of Jesus and made it the capital city of Galilee. The construction of a lavish city on a virgin site is reminiscent of the building done by his father. But there was a reason that no one had built upon this site before; it was the site of a cemetery. This may explain why compulsion became a necessary tool in finding residents for the city.[34] Following the destruction of Jerusalem in AD 70, the best Jewish scholars were forced to flee Jerusalem as it became a city totally dedicated to the pagan culture of Rome. Many of these scholars settled in Tiberias where the Jewish Talmud came into being (AD 400) and the Hebrew consonantal text was given formal, vowel-sound marking by the Ben Asher family (AD 700–1,000).[35]

1. Sand dunes on the shoreline of the Mediterranean Sea.

2. The Philistine Plain.

3.
Travel is difficult
in the mountains
of Upper Galilee.

4. The agricultural valleys of Lower Galilee.

5. The Jezreel Valley looking east toward Mount Carmel.

6. The Lebonah Valley in Samaria.

7. A rainfall shadow over eastern Samaria produces a chalk desert.

8. Shechem lies in the valley between Mount Ebal (right)
and Mount Gerizim (left).

9. Mountain groups cluster in Samaria.

10. Jacob's Well at Sychar (John 4).

11. The Bejamin Plateau.

12. Narrow, V-shaped valleys bisect the Judean Highlands.

13. Threshing floor near Bethlehem with shepherd's fields
in the background.

14. A cave functions as a sheepfold near Bethlehem.

15. Low, rolling hills rise above wide, U-shaped valleys
in the Elah Valley (Shephelah).

16. The southern end of the Dead Sea
and the Mountains of Moab.

17. St. George's Monastery in the Judean Wilderness.

18. The Negev Basin.

19. Foundation of an Israelite (four-room) house at Beersheba.

20. The Wilderness of Zin.

21.
The Timnah
Mountains in the
southern reaches of
the Arabah.

22.
Headwaters of the
Jordan River near
Dan.

23.
The Jordan
River.

24.
Rising terrain
on the east
shore of the Sea
of Galilee.

25. The Sea of Galilee looking north from its southern shore.

26. Wildflowers in the Jordan Valley just below the mountain ridge rising to form the eastern plateau.

27.
Jesus taught on the site
of this synagogue in
Capernaum.

28.
Cave number 4 at
Qumran, home of
the Dead Sea Scrolls.

29. Grapes are grown close to the ground in a Judean field.

30. A beam press (reconstruction) at Hazor.

31. Camels provided reliable, long-distance transportation
under harsh desert conditions.

32. A view north into the broken and rugged terrain
of Upper Galilee.

10

THE JORDAN RIVER
AND THE DEAD SEA

lthough the rift valley begins far to the north, the most dramatic
images of this region are reserved for the one traveling the Lower
Jordan Valley. Water gathering from the tributaries that feed the
Jordan River conspires with the topography to turn the ancient river into
a series of whitewater rapids. The waters of the Jordan seethed and
churned before quietly entering the deathly calm of the Dead Sea.

This Lower Jordan Valley plays a role in a number of Bible stories. For
example, in the Old Testament the water of this river stood as a barrier
between the advancing army of Israel and the Promised Land. Jericho
stood near the river at a ford guarding access to the land of Canaan. As
Joshua led the Israelites toward Jericho, the river miraculously stopped
flowing from upstream. This divine act is striking given its historical and
theological symmetry. Earlier in Israel's history, the Lord had opened the
gate of the Red Sea allowing the Israelites to leave Egypt by walking
through a dry seabed. Now as they conclude their time in the wilderness,
the Lord opens another gate, the Jordan River, to allow the Israelite army
to cross on dry ground. This historical symmetry carries with it the theological security of the Lord's presence and power. Once safely across the
river, Joshua and the Israelites travel only a few miles before observing
that powerful presence at work again. The residents of Jericho knew that
they were about to be attacked so they had prepared for an Israelite siege.

Because a siege might last for months, the residents had barricaded themselves and their supplies behind thick doors and stout walls. But it was just a few days before the walls of Jericho collapsed before blaring trumpets and the shouts of Israelite soldiers.

The New Testament writers also speak of events connected with the Jordan River, such as where the forerunner of Jesus preached and taught. John the Baptist proclaimed a message of repentance that included an invitation to be baptized in the water of the Jordan River. Though the Son of God was the creator of this water, Jesus asked John to baptize Him with that water, signaling the beginning of his public ministry among us. Clearly the more we learn about this region, the more we will know about such stories. And so we begin our walk through the Lower Jordan Valley.

Boundaries and Dimensions

The Lower Jordan Valley begins at the southern end of the Sea of Galilee and continues south until reaching the Dead Sea. If we were to draw a straight line on a map between these two points, we would measure a direct distance of 65 miles. Over the course of this distance, the valley floor widens and narrows as the mountain boundaries intrude and retreat from its center. Just south of the Sea of Galilee, the mountains of Lower Galilee on the west and Gilead on the east press in to make the valley approximately 4 miles wide. At Beth Shan, the valley opens to approximately 7 miles. But 10 miles south of Beth Shan, the mountains of Samaria and Gilead compress the valley to a width of only 2 miles. And so the valley remains before widening to its broadest dimensions at Jericho where the valley floor extends for 14 miles.

Topography

When viewed in cross section, we see that the Lower Jordan Valley is actually composed of three different valleys, each housed within the other. These subdivisions are called the Zor, the Qattara, and the Ghor. The innermost valley is the Zor, and is the channel in which the Jordan River actually flows. This valley is approximately 200 yards wide and up to 150 feet below the Qattara.[1] In the northern stretches of the Lower Jordan Valley, the Zor is filled by a shoulder-high dense thicket of tamarisk, oleander, willows, poplar, vines, thorns, and thistles.[2] Through the middle of the Zor and below its muddy banks the Jordan River itself meanders. (See photo 23.) This ancient riverbed is very serpentine, twisting and turning back and forth on itself. We noted that the direct distance from the Sea of Galilee to the Dead Sea is 65 miles. But the riverbed more than doubles that distance as it flows for 135 miles on its way to the Dead Sea. During biblical times, the water averaged from 90 to 100 feet in width. But during the spring floods, the river would have flowed out of the Zor and expanded the river surface to nearly a mile in places. The average depth of the river varied from 3 feet at the natural fords up to 13 feet in the heart of the channel.[3]

As we walk from the Jordan riverbed toward the rising terrain on either side of the Zor, we next encounter the Qattara. The Qattara begins about 17 miles south of the Sea of Galilee and continues to the Dead Sea.[4] It looks like a miniature badlands because it is composed of Lisan marl that resists the penetration of water and is devoid of all vegetation.[5] Beyond the Qattara and reaching to the base of the hills on either side of the Jordan Valley is the Ghor. The Ghor has soils favorable for the growing of crops and for the pasturing of animals. Because the northern and eastern portions of the Ghor receive more annual precipitation, they have the greenest presentation.

The entire Lower Jordan Valley tilts down toward the Dead Sea. On average, the river descends at a rate of 9 feet per mile. The most dramatic loss in elevation occurs in the first 15 miles below the Sea of Galilee. There, the river drops at a rate of 40 feet per mile.[6] This dramatic drop in elevation gave the river its name. The name Jordan derives from a Hebrew verb that means "to descend." The Jordan River is certainly a river marked by its dramatic rate of descent.

During the biblical period, water that exited the south end of the Sea of Galilee was joined by water that rushed from significant tributaries that brought runoff water from the mountains of Gilead. The most significant contribution to the hydrologic flow is made by the Yarmuk and the Jabbok Rivers. That volume of water, coupled with the dramatic drop in altitude over the course of the river's journey, results in more than a few whitewater rapids. In 1848 United States explorer W. F. Lynch reported encounters with twenty-seven whitewater rapids in his float trip on the Jordan River from the Sea of Galilee to the Dead Sea. This experienced river runner wrote in his journal: "To my consternation, I soon found that the Jordan was interrupted in its course by frequent and most fearful

rapids . . . placing our sole trust in Providence, we plunged with head-
long velocity down appalling descents."[7] The speed and force of the current means that the river would cut into the banks, scrape soil from
those banks, and mix it into the water. This process gives the Jordan its
characteristic muddy appearance. Naaman, the Aramean commander
who had leprosy, nearly walked away from the miraculous healing
offered to him by Elisha when he was put off by the appearance of the
river. He would rather have washed himself off in the crystal clear waters
flowing from the mountains in Damascus than the muddy water of the
Jordan River (2 Kings 5:11–12).

Culture

The number of people actually living in the Lower Jordan Valley during
the biblical period was very small. Malaria-filled swampland, high temperatures, and risk of attack by wild animals conspired to prevent significant settlement here. Some agriculture was possible in the northern portions of the valley where increased rainfall and water from the tributaries
might be tapped for irrigation.[8] But generally, the Jordan River is too low
in elevation and becomes too laden with chemicals to be valuable for irrigation. This is particularly true in the southern stretches of the valley
where the salinity of the soil is so high that it prevents any success with
agriculture at all.[9]

Typically, valleys provide desirable transportation routes, but the Jordan Valley was not as extensively used as one might expect. The river itself
was not navigable by the ancients due to the whitewater rapids.[10] Those
that traveled on foot faced the significant travel risks that are associated
with this valley. During the summer travel season, the temperatures in this
valley can become oppressive and extreme. For example, the average daily
high in Jericho during the month of August is 102 degrees.[11] As the valley
lies at such a low elevation, compression of the air in the valley, as well as
the absence of a cooling sea breeze, can weary the traveler quickly, and
increase the likelihood of dehydration.

While this is particularly true in the southern portion of the valley, the
northern portion had threats and obstacles of its own. Jeremiah com-
ments on the difficulty posed by the dense thickets when he asks, "If you
stumble in safe country, how will you manage in the thickets by the Jordan?" (Jeremiah 12:5). The pools of water that can form in the northern

portions of the valley offer a paradise for birds like the stork, starling, heron, and egret.[12] But these same pools breed mosquitoes infected with malaria. Wild animals also were more prevalent in the Zor, which raised concerns for the traveler who could encounter lions, wild boars, leopards, and wolves.[13] This risk was so real that Jeremiah could use it in a metaphor to describe the Lord's coming judgment on Moab. "Like a lion coming up from Jordan's thickets to a rich pastureland, I will chase Edom from its land in an instant" (Jeremiah 49:19).

Despite these risks, travelers did use the valley for short stretches. This is particularly true of travelers who were moving from east to west across the Jordan River. The typical traveler would plan to cross the river at one of the natural fords because there were no bridges.[14] Once the traveler had crossed the river, the Jordan Valley was used only to get to another travel artery that ran outside the valley. Of course, this meant that important fords like those opposite Jericho and Beth Shan became key points for controlling access into or out of the land. When Ehud was fighting the Moabites and wanted to prevent them from getting back home safely, he ordered his men to seize the fords, which resulted in a great victory for Israel (Judges 3:28–30). In the same way, administrative cities that would harbor both tax collectors and soldiers were built at these key fords to harvest taxes from traders and to guard these points of access against military invasion.

Biblical History

Joshua and the Israelites also had to cross the Jordan River in order to enter the Promised Land. He prepared the people for invasion on the Plains of Moab that lie on the east side of the Jordan River, just north of the Dead Sea, and opposite the city of Jericho. A military crossing of the Jordan River, even at a ford like that opposite Jericho, was risky because the soldiers would be more vulnerable during the time it took to cross the river. Because the Jordan River was at flood stage (Joshua 3:15), a swifter current, deeper water, and longer crossing would create even more exposure for the advancing army. But just as the Lord intervened with a water miracle as the Israelites left Egypt, so the Lord promises Joshua that He will open the waters of the Jordan River so that the military might cross over on dry ground (Joshua 3:13). When the priests who were carrying the ark of the covenant reached the water of the Jordan, the water stopped flowing from upstream and piled up miles to the north at Adam (Joshua 3:15–16). The manner in which the inspired author reports this event suggests that the Lord may have produced this miracle by manipulating an otherwise natural occurrence. On occasion, large blocks of Lisan from the Qattara have broken away and temporarily blocked the flow of the Jordan River. For example, in 1547 the river was blocked for two days, in 1906 for ten hours, and in 1927 for 27 hours.[15] However the Lord chose to do it, the miracle's value extended well beyond this day. Eventually, coalitions of Canaanite cities would gather to repulse the invasion of Joshua and the Israelites. But at the crucial, initial stage of the invasion, this miracle evaporated the courage of the opposition, and gave the Israelites the opportunity to gain a critical foothold in the land (Joshua 5:1).

Centuries later, water from the Jordan Valley would again play an important role in the history of our salvation. This story begins with Jesus leaving Galilee in pursuit of John, for He intended to use the baptism of John in a very important way. The exact location of Jesus' baptism is uncertain. John 1:28 implies that it was near the village of Bethany on the east side of the Jordan. Some have placed this Bethany near the Wadi el-Kharrar about 6 miles east of Jericho,[16] while others have placed it several miles to the north near the Yarmuk River.[17] At the moment, there is not enough evidence to identify the location conclusively. What is certain is that John was baptizing on the east side of the Lower Jordan Valley. And in this valley, the appearance of the Holy Spirit in the form of a dove and the announcement of the Father made it clear that Jesus' public ministry had begun (Matthew 3:16–17).

THE DEAD SEA

Boundaries and Dimensions

The Jordan River terminates in one of the most unique and unusual bodies of water on the face of the earth, the Dead Sea. This body of water is also called the Salt Sea (Genesis 14:3), the Sea of the Arabah (Deuteronomy 3:17), and the Eastern Sea (since it lies east of Jerusalem, Ezekiel 47:18). It resides in a large bowl set between the mountains of the Judean Wilderness that rise 1,300 feet above the west shore of the lake and the Mountains of Moab that rise 2,500–3,000 feet above the east shore. The

Dead Sea is Israel's largest inland body of water, and includes a lakebed that is approximately 53 miles long and 10 miles wide. But the area actually occupied by water can vary by a mile or more from year to year due to changes in rainfall and evaporation rate. The lake itself is an elongated oval with a peninsula of land called the Lisan (Arabic for "tongue") protruding into the lake from the east. (See photo 16.) The Lisan divides the southern third of the lake from the rest of the water. During extreme drought conditions, the water between the Lisan and the west shore of the Dead Sea, called the Lynch Straits, can actually dry up and create two separate bodies of water. This happened as recently as 1976.[18] The northern portion of the lake, with the lakebed lying 1,300 feet below the surface, is considerably deeper than the southern third. Soundings in the north indicate that the bottom of the lake lies 1,300 feet below the surface while the southern third has a depth of only 25 feet.[19] The shore around the lake is desolate. When Lynch arrived there, he wrote, "There was virtually no vegetation whatever; barren mountains, fragments or rocks blackened by sulfurous deposits . . . dead trees upon its margins. All within the scope of vision bore a sad and somber aspect."[20]

Topography

The Dead Sea basin is where the Afro-Arabian Fault Line reaches its deepest penetration into the earth. If we drill from there toward the core of the earth, we will not strike bedrock until we are 23,000 feet below the surface.[21] Standing on the shore, upon thousands of feet of unconsolidated fill, we are standing at the lowest point on the earth's surface; 1,290 feet below sea level. Interestingly, the visitor standing there is actually 1,300 feet below the visitor standing just 50 miles to the west on the shore of the Mediterranean Sea. There has been some discussion of using this elevation difference to generate electrical power. Water taken from the Mediterranean Sea would be piped to the Dead Sea, and the force of the water en route would be used to turn electricity-producing turbines. No apparent progress, however, has been made on this immense public works project.

Geology

The Dead Sea is not only the lowest point on the earth's surface, but it is also the most chemical body of water on earth, due in part to the composition of the sea's basin that is heavy in naturally occurring substances. For example, Har Sedom (the Mountain of Salt) that lies astride the Dead Sea is a 7-mile long by 2-mile wide mountain of solid rock salt. Streams feeding the Dead Sea become increasingly chemical as they course through this kind of terrain. What is more, openings in the bottom of the sea pump in sulphur, bromine, magnesium, potassium, calcium, and iodine from underlying fault crevices.[22] Bitumen (petroleum hardened by evaporation and oxidation) can also be found in the lake.[23] When the Romans saw the black, tar-like chunks floating to the surface of the lake, they gave the sea its Roman name, Lake of Asphalt.[24]

The predominant chemical in the lake is salt, which makes this the most saline body of water on earth. While the ocean typically boasts a salt content of 3.5 percent, the Dead Sea has a salt content of up to 33 percent. This, of course, means that the marine life we typically associate with an inland lake is not able to survive in this water. Hundreds of tourists still visit the shores of the Dead Sea today, hoping to "float" on the water because the salt makes it impossible for them to sink. An object will float in water when the weight of the water displaced by the object is greater than the weight of the object itself. That is why a heavy ocean liner will float but a coin will sink. In both fresh and ocean water, humans are not buoyant enough to float unaided because the weight of the water we displace is not more than our own body weight. This is not true with the water in the Dead Sea. Volume for volume, Dead Sea water is heavier than seawater. Consequently, it is possible to step into the Dead Sea and float without kicking or treading water.

Natural Resources

The water that arrives in the Dead Sea typically arrives from the rivers and springs flowing into it rather than from precipitation. The rainfall in the Dead Sea basin varies from 4 inches in the north to only 2 inches in the south. This, of course, would not be sufficient to produce such a large lake. The rest of the water is provided by a catchment basin of over 11,000 square miles from which an additional seven million tons of water arrives in the Dead Sea each year.[25] That water has no place to go but up. Given the low elevation of this sea, it has no natural outlet. The only way water leaves is by evaporation. On a typical summer day, up to one-half inch of water can evaporate from the lake's surface.[26]

That evaporation is due to the extreme temperatures in the basin. The average high temperature during the summer is 95 degrees, but some summer days reach temperatures as high as 125 degrees. The high temperatures are due to the lack of cloud cover, absence of cooling breezes from the Mediterranean, geothermal heating, and the low elevation at which the lake resides. At 1,300 feet below sea level, the atmosphere at the lake's surface is compressed much more than that at sea level and compressed air produces heat. When you use a hand pump to put air into a basketball or bike tire, the bottom of the pump gets warm because you are compressing the air within the pump. The same thing happens at the Dead Sea. Because of the low elevation, the air molecules at the surface are carrying the additional weight of the atmosphere above them. This higher air pressure results in more oxygen at the surface (6–8 percent more than at sea level) and much warmer temperatures.[27]

Culture

The rigor of living in the Dead Sea basin prevented significant urbanization. Nevertheless, this region did have a unique contribution to make to culture and society. The precipitous Mountains of Moab to the east prevented any road from forming on the east shore of the lake. But a small plain on the west side of the lake did allow for some north-south transportation and access to the trails that led west through the Judean Wilderness. A walk on those trails reveals that there are very few green plants that grow naturally in the Dead Sea basin except near the occasional freshwater spring. Near such springs, like those at En Gedi, farmers tended plantations of date palms and balsam trees that thrived on the fresh water.[28]

The Dead Sea region also provided an inviting winter climate. While the summer temperatures were nearly unbearable, the milder winter temperatures, averaging 68 degrees, were ideal when compared with the cold winter temperatures in the mountains around Jerusalem. So if you lived in the mountains and had sufficient wealth, you might have a winter home like King Herod did in Jericho. King Herod also took advantage of another natural resource associated with the Dead Sea; hot water baths. For example, we know that he came to the hot springs at Callirrhoe during the last days of his life to ease the pain of his horrible illness.[29]

Industry associated with the Dead Sea focused on the harvesting of natural resources in the area. Salt was harvested from the region and shipped north to cities on the Sea of Galilee like Magdala, where it was used to process and preserve the fish taken from the sea. Salt was also used for seasoning foods in much the same way we use salt today (Job 6:6). Thoughtful businessmen also saw a market for the bitumen that floated to the surface on the Dead Sea. They would use reed rafts to collect this petroleum product and then sell it to those who were waterproofing their boats. This product also made its way to Egypt via camel because the Egyptian embalming process required the use of bitumen.[30] Finally, if you were not interested in the Dead Sea for its winter climate, hot baths, or industry, you might come for the solitude. The separatist community at Qumran found some measure of isolation from the rest of the world here.

Biblical History

Two cities associated with the Dead Sea invite further comment, Jericho and Qumran. While the Old and New Testament Jericho are found in two different locations, they are located closely enough to share the same geographical environment. Jericho is located approximately 7 miles north of the Dead Sea and 5 miles west of the Jordan River on the edge of the Judean Wilderness. Jericho is both the lowest city on the earth's surface (821 feet below sea level) as well as the oldest city on record with continuous occupation to the present. The earliest archaeological evidence suggests that people were living in Jericho as early as the eighth millennium BC. That is approximately 5,000 years before Abraham entered the land.

Since biblical times, people have been drawn to Jericho because of its location and natural resources. The most critical need faced by any resident of the Promised Land was water. Jericho has Elisha's Spring (following 2 Kings 2:19–22) that gushes water at a rate of 1,200 gallons per minute.[31] This water meets all the household needs of Jericho's residents and creates an opportunity for agriculture to thrive in the desert. That agriculture includes fruit, grain, spices, and products associated with the date palm. The date palm is what gives the city the nickname "City of Palms" (Deuteronomy 34:3; Judges 3:13; 2 Chronicles 28:15). The date palm is the premier plant of the desert oasis and grows to a height of more than 55 feet with branches that extend 7 to 10 feet.[32] The date itself is harvested at the end of summer and used to make fruit, honey (called dibs), and juice. Each of these products is a great source of energy.[33] The leaves and branches of the palm were also harvested and used to produce mats, baskets, and other household items.[34] As noted above, the minerals harvested from the Dead Sea were also of value in the ancient world. The residents of ancient Jericho often mined salt and bitumen as a source of income.

While the natural resources made Jericho livable, its location made it desirable. Jericho would be the first city that the Israelites would attack, and geography played a role in that decision. The Old Testament city of Jericho was not particularly large. The floor plan, as reflected in the archaeological record, suggests that it was an average-sized walled city of about 7 acres. It was obviously not the size of ancient Jericho that made it a strategic target, but its critical location that demanded the attention of the Israelite invasion.[35] Jericho guarded a critical ford that allowed for easier passage across the Jordan River. It also was the gate that guarded access to Benjamin. Recall that the Benjamin Plateau functions as the internal crossroads of the hill country. That is why Joshua sent spies ahead to assess the defensive capability of the city (Joshua 2), and that is certainly one of the reasons that the Lord brought about its total destruction (Joshua 6).

The strategic setting of the city also sheds light on the striking demand placed upon Israel after Jericho had fallen. In Joshua 6:26, the Lord instructs Israel not to rebuild the city. Once Israel possessed the land, the location of Jericho would still have functioned as a key geographical gate. The natural ford leading to the heartland of Benjamin would have led Israel's enemies to attack along the same route that Joshua did. Yet the Lord asks Israel to step out in faith and allow Him to guard the eastern frontier rather than erect a fortification here. Apparently the Israelites honored this request for centuries because the next record we have of a city built in this location is from the time of King Ahab. Companioned with Jezebel, Ahab is arguably the worst king to lead God's people. And it was during his reign that the city of Jericho was rebuilt (1 Kings 16:34). The inspired author surely mentions the rebuilding of this city during his reign because it is a symbol of the apostasy displayed during the administration of Ahab.

The New Testament city of Jericho is found to the west of the Old Testament city of Jericho. This city, dominated by the winter home of King Herod the Great, was the city in which Jesus ministered and taught. Here, Jesus heals blind men (Matthew 20:29–34) and goes to the home of a tax collector named Zacchaeus (Luke 19:1–10) after calling him from the branches of a sycamore tree. This man, who was shorter than most, grew significantly that day, for Jesus declared him to be a son of Abraham due to the faith that blossomed in his heart.

The other city that invites brief mention is Qumran, which was made famous by the discovery of the Dead Sea Scrolls in the area. Although formally unmentioned in the Bible, it does offer unique insights into the culture and social structure of the biblical period. Qumran is located just a few miles to the south of Jericho and just above the shoreline of the Dead Sea. The first residents used Qumran as a lookout post as early as the eighth century BC[36] because it offered a commanding view of the Dead Sea's northern shore. But little evidence remains of this Israelite community other than the watchtower itself. Years later, during the Intertestimental Period, a new community was founded here. Beginning in 1947, the world began to glimpse documents associated with that community. These documents were unearthed in the caves near the ruin called Qumran, a discovery that once again put this city on the map of public attention. Ancient authors wrote about a group of people living on the northeast side of the Dead Sea, whom they called the Essenes, and modern scholars began to link them both to the ruin and the scrolls. Thus, it was assumed that the ruin of Qumran was inhabited by the Essenes and that the Essenes were the ones who had written the Dead Sea Scrolls. While some have disputed this conclusion, the scholarly consensus at the moment assumes the Essenes lived there and wrote the documents discovered in the caves. (See photo 28.) The Essenes were a conservative Jewish group that broke away from mainstream Judaism and the worship in Jerusalem they deemed corrupt. They retreated to Qumran during the silent time between the Old and New Testament to live a more isolated life where they could practice their religious life as they wished. The Dead Sea Scrolls present the theology and practices of their community. Those scrolls include the verbatim copying of Old Testament passages, commentaries on the Old Testament books, and documents that describe their rules and beliefs as a community.

The visitor who walks around the archaeological site of Qumran will be impressed by the number of baths and cisterns present in the ruin. Water was clearly important both for the fundamental needs of life and for ritual practice. The spring of Ein Feshkha was close enough to provide for a portion of their freshwater needs. But this community's water needs went beyond that, so a dam was constructed. After the winter storms, this dam would divert rushing water from pursuing a path from the Judean Wilderness to the Dead Sea.[37] Then the water was directed by various channels to the large cisterns and baths located throughout the Qumran ruin.

So there was life along the Dead Sea, but not in the Dead Sea. That is why it served as such a dramatic image in Ezekiel's message about a time of restoration. In his vision, the Messianic age will be one in which the barren shores of the Dead Sea would be full of trees, and the water would become fresh and be filled with large numbers of fish (Ezekiel 47:6–12). That language clearly illustrates how dramatically the world can change when the Gospel is preached and faith takes root in the hearts of believers.

11

THE SOUTHERN WILDERNESS

South of the Dead Sea, the landscape of the Promised Land becomes even more harsh and forbidding. The geographic realities are so dire that they threaten to take the life of anyone who would challenge them by setting foot in this environment. In the modern state of Israel, land is an extremely precious commodity. Land costs are very high and residents are ready to fight both with words and fists for the rights to even a small piece of property. But even in this modern context, the desert regions we are about to discuss remain largely unsettled. In fact, this southern wilderness offers an environment so harsh that even the hardy Bedouin penetrate no further than the edges where they find forage for their animals. This land is the great southern desert that extends from the south end of the Dead Sea to the Red Sea; an area that the biblical authors divide into three main areas. These are the Arabah, the Wilderness of Zin, and the Wilderness of Paran. We will explore each of the areas individually and see that this division is justified by subtle variations in the geography of each.

Given the austerity of the southern desert, we would expect to see few biblical events set in this region, and that expectation proves true. While we do hear of settlement in places like Ezion Geber and Kadesh Barnea, these are the exceptions. For the most part, this wilderness is not settled by Israelites, only used by them during times of transition. The most striking example of transitional time in the desert occurs at the time of Moses. After leading the Israelites from Egypt to Mount Sinai, the Lord brings the

Israelites through the southern desert and detains them in the Wilderness of Zin for nearly 40 years. Our visit here will be much more brief. But though our stay is short, it will be full of information that illuminates this time in Israel's history and the miracles used to sustain them there.

ARABAH

Boundaries and Dimensions

Our trip through the southern desert will begin with the Arabah. In the Old Testament, the term *Arabah* is used to describe that portion of the rift valley that extends from the Sea of Galilee to the Red Sea (1 Samuel 23:24), often referring specifically to the northern portions of that valley (as in Deuteronomy 3:17). But here, we use the term for the desert valley that extends 105 miles southward from the Dead Sea to the Red Sea. The width of the valley varies between 4 and 15 miles. The valley is enclosed by the mountains of Edom on the east and the rising hills of the desert to the west, which intrude into and withdraw from the valley floor.

Topography and Geology

The Arabah has a flat and valley-like appearance for most of its run. It begins over 1,000 feet below sea level at the Dead Sea before rising to its maximum elevation of 1,160 feet above sea level, 62 miles south of the Dead Sea. From there, it descends again to sea level at the Gulf of Eilat.[1]

The valley floor is littered with sand, brackish soil, and gravel. For the first 25 miles south of the Dead Sea, the Arabah is a severely desiccated badlands composed of marl and salt.[2] But farther to the south, alluvial sand and gravel predominate the valley floor. The flow of the valley is interrupted at regular intervals by alluvial fans of gravel that have been washed down from higher elevations as a consequence of flash floods.[3] These fans are thickest and widest on the eastern side of the Arabah due to the more significant rains experienced by the Mountains of Edom. At various places in the valley, visitors' eyes are drawn to places where the duller limestone gives way to red Nubian sandstone. These bright outcroppings of color are particularly evident near Punom and Timna.

Natural Resources

Sustaining life in the Arabah is as difficult as anywhere in Israel. As always, water is a concern. But here it takes on a particular urgency due to the very low precipitation totals seen by the region. Most of this valley receives less than 2 inches of annual precipitation, and that amount falls during just a few weeks of the year.[4] As people need water to survive, it is the wells and springs that are the key to existence in this valley. Those wells and springs are particularly numerous on the east side of the valley where the higher Mountains of Edom force more moisture from the air. Flash floods that course down these mountains into the Arabah do not have a chance to form a river that travels the full distance to the Dead Sea or the Red Sea because the gravel fans block the progress along the valley floor. Rather, the water whose flow is slowed by these alluvial fans either evaporates or soaks down into the ground. This is the groundwater that supplies the wells and springs that make life possible in the Arabah.[5] Given the small amount of precipitation, this valley that has few springs also has very little vegetation. Placing a typical portion of the valley underneath a grid, we find only one plant in every dozen or so square meters.[6] In reality, the number of plants on the valley floor is so small that a walk through the valley gives the impression there are no plants at all except for the occasional acacia tree.

Culture

The dry and forbidding quality of this valley limits both its permanent habitation and its practical use by those who do live there. The main economic importance of this valley is associated with copper and trade. Where the bright Nubian sandstone makes its appearance in the Arabah, copper is often present. Thus it is no surprise that the red-orange sandstone near Punom and Timna was aggressively mined by the ancients for copper.[7] (See photo 21.)

Like any valley in the Promised Land, the Arabah also supported some measure of transportation. This long north-south valley did not rival the other major roadways along the Mediterranean Sea and along the watershed of the Mountains of Edom. But the Arabah did serve as a point of connection between those two more popular roadways. In the east, the Arabah connected with the King's Highway via a road starting at Petra. Alternatively, those moving west would travel the road through Tamar and Beersheba en route to the International Highway.[8]

Biblical History

The Arabah was likely used as a roadway by the Israelites after the Edomites refused them direct passage to the King's Highway. The Israelites had requested permission to use that highway on their way to the Promised Land, and vowed that they would not consume any of their food or drink any water for which they did not pay (Numbers 20:14–19). Nevertheless, Edom refused them passage, so they were forced to make a 175-mile detour traveling south through the Arabah toward the Red Sea in order to travel around Edom (Numbers 21:4; Deuteronomy 2:8).

The one city associated with that trip that also appears on other pages of the Bible is Ezion Geber. Ezion Geber lies on the coast of the Red Sea at the southern end of the Arabah. What at first glance might appear to be an ideal location for a harbor proves to be disappointing for the ancient mariners. The predominantly northern winds and narrow gulf made it difficult for ships under sail to tack effectively northward.[9] What is more, storms that generated winds of more than 50 miles per hour and treacherous coral reefs threatened both the cargo and lives of the sailors. Nevertheless, this was Israel's opportunity for maritime access to eastern Egypt, Africa, and India. Thus Solomon constructed a seaport and fleet at this location with the assistance of the more experienced seamen of Phoenicia (2 Chronicles 8:17–18). Centuries later, the modern Israeli city of Eilat stands in approximately the same location as Solomon's seaport. The deep waters of the Red Sea associated with the Gulf of Eilat make it a major seaport for the modern state of Israel. The Gulf of Eilat provides a great economic resource as well as a natural wonder. The unique combination of water temperature and sea life forms the most dramatic underwater coral reefs in the world. Scuba divers from throughout the world flock to Eilat to get a glimpse of these pristine reefs and the aquatic life inhabiting them.

THE WILDERNESS OF ZIN AND THE WILDERNESS OF PARAN

Boundaries and Dimensions

To the west of the Arabah lies the extensive wilderness that the biblical authors describe with two names, the Wilderness of Zin and the Wilderness of Paran. These regions that stretch from the biblical Negev toward the Red Sea have borders that are less clearly defined. The Wilderness of Zin lies to the north of Kadesh Barnea and extends to the Negev. The Wilderness of Zin extends from Kadesh Barnea (Numbers 12:3 and 21) southward toward the traditional location of Mount Sinai. While these two regions share a number of geographical characteristics, their division from each other is justified by the differences in topography.

Topography and Geology

The Wilderness of Zin presents a series of parallel ridges that run from southwest to northeast paralleling the shoreline of the Mediterranean Sea.[10] The elevation of these ridges varies with the highest point being Har Ramon that climbs to 3,396 feet above sea level. Many of these ridges are asymmetric in shape with the northwest face having a gentler slope and the southeastern face presenting a much steeper slope.[11] (See photo 20.)

By contrast, the Wilderness of Paran has a more plateau-like appearance. The flat or slightly rolling landscape of Paran is drained by many broad and shallow wadis. These riverbeds are dry most of the year. But when it does rain, they carry the water collected from numerous tributaries towards the Arabah. In walking through such a wadi, you would find it filled by silt, rocks, and some boulders. Perhaps the most striking topographical features of both regions are the large craters called makhteshim. These extensive craters have both a very majestic and forbidding appearance to them with walls that can rise vertically to over 1,300 feet above the crater floor.

Culture

The harsh terrain we find in the Wilderness of Zin and Wilderness of Paran is amplified by the lack of vegetation. Even grasses are a scarce commodity in the region due to the very small amount of annual rainfall. The Wilderness of Zin receives only 4–8 inches of precipitation and the Wilderness of Paran receives only 1–2 inches of precipitation each year. The austerity of natural resources has severely limited the establishment of human residence in the region. As Beitzel has observed, "This region is generally hostile to human activities, and not even bedouin flocks can find satisfactory grazing in its barren rocklands."[12]

Biblical History

As we have noted above, very little biblical history actually occurs in this region. While that is true, the Wilderness of Zin and the Wilderness of Paran are the settings for an extended stay of the Israelites presented to us in the Book of Numbers. An awareness of the geography in this region will dramatically enhance our reading of this segment of biblical history.

After the Israelites had spent 400 years in Egypt, God brought them to Mount Sinai. He then led them via the Mount Seir Road (Deuteronomy 1:2), through the Wilderness of Paran (Numbers 10:12), and to the Wilderness of Zin (Numbers 14). A reconnaissance mission was sent from Kadesh Barnea into the Promised Land in order to build a passion for the next step in God's plan (Numbers 13:1–25). That mission was to include a significant survey of the geography including water, agriculture, and urbanization (Numbers 13:17–20). But eight members of the reconnaissance team misrepresented the geography in a way that robbed people of their passion for entering the land.[13] Because Israel failed to trust in God's promises, the adult members of that community who failed to trust were sentenced to die in this wilderness during the next decades. It would be their children who would enter the Promised Land (Numbers 14:30–35).

Despite this failure to trust the Lord, He did not abandon Israel in the desert, but rather provided one miracle after another to sustain them there. When Jeremiah criticized the Israelites of his day for failing to remember the gracious acts of God in their lives, he said that they had become like their fathers who failed to remember God's loving-kindness. It is at this point that Jeremiah calls attention to the harsh geographic conditions in which their fathers lived. "What fault did your fathers find in Me, that they strayed so far from Me? They followed worthless idols and became worthless themselves. They did not ask, 'Where is the LORD, who brought us up out of Egypt and led us through the barren wilderness, through a land of deserts and rifts, a land of drought and darkness, a land where no one travels and no one lives?'" (Jeremiah 2:5–6).

Those acts of divine love are closely linked to the food and water that the Israelites needed to survive in this harsh ecosystem. When the Israelites were complaining about the lack of food, God provided manna for them in addition to supplementing their meat supply. As God provided water for the Israelites at Mount Sinai (Exodus 17:1–7) so He provided water for them in the Wilderness of Zin (Numbers 20:1–13).

Two things become apparent when we apply our knowledge of geography to these wilderness stories. First, it is absolutely clear that without divine intervention, the people of Israel and the promise of the Savior connected to their bloodline would have died in the wilderness. There is simply not enough water or food to sustain even a small population for a short period of time, much less thousands of people living for decades. These miracles of God were not about entertainment, they were about survival. Second, only a few miracles that detail the provision of food and water are recorded for us by the inspired writer. Given the number of years that people were in this wilderness, the nature of its geography, and the substantial number of people to sustain, this cannot be a comprehensive record of divine provision. Many more miracles would have accompanied the daily manna in order to sustain this community. Thus, we may read the stories of divine provision as examples of God's intervention rather than a comprehensive listing of such acts. The truth of the matter is that we must multiply these miracles many times over during these forty years in order to get an accurate picture of the divine intervention that sustained Israel.

But it was during one of these miracles that a striking change in the status of Moses occurred. Recall that Moses had been called and trained by God to lead the Israelites out of Egypt to Mount Sinai and then into the Promised Land. But during one of the water-provision miracles, Moses disqualified himself from entering the Promised Land. The sin of Moses is clearly linked to the geography. This event begins when the people come to him with a complaint about the geography. "Why did you bring us up out of Egypt to this terrible place? It has no grain or figs, grapevines or pomegranates. And there is no water to drink!" (Numbers 20:5). At this point, the Lord instructs Moses to provide water for the people by "speaking" to a rock. This is a different directive than Moses had received years earlier (Exodus 17) when he had been instructed to "strike" a rock. Moses proceeds to strike the rock instead of speaking to it. Water pours from the rock and Moses is told that his sin has disqualified him from leading Israel into the Promised Land.

Why did this act disqualify Moses as the leader of Israel? Once again, geography provides us with a clue. The miracle of Exodus 17, where Moses was instructed to strike a rock, and the miracles of Numbers 20, where Moses was instructed to speak to the rock, occur in very different geological environments. In Exodus 17, Moses and the Israelites are in southern Sinai camped at Rephidim. The rock in this region is all granite. This metamorphic rock is very densely composed and does not absorb any water. To strike this rock and have it bring forth water would have been a great miracle and glory would have been given to God.

By contrast, the Wilderness of Zin is composed of an upper layer of porous chalk over layers of less permeable limestone. Rain that fell in the area would be absorbed by the chalk and directed down by gravity. When this water met the boundary between the chalk and limestone, gravity would force the water to flow horizontally toward an exit point. It is at those points that we see water leeching from the rock in the Wilderness of Zin. But as the rainwater moved through the upper story of chalk, it would dissolve some of the chalk and transport it to the point where the water seeped out of the rock face. Evaporation at the exit point would leave behind crystals that had dissolved in the water. These crystals would eventually form a mineral cap that prevented any more water from flowing out of this rock. Of course, that did not mean that water would stop collecting behind that mineral cap. This hidden water resource awaited the blow from a shrewd water seeker who knew how to read the rock. A sharp blow on this mineral cap would cause water to flow from a rock.[14]

Consider again God's instructions to Moses. He told Moses to speak to the rock. When Moses lashed out and struck the rock as he did at Rephidim, his action would not produce the same result. In Exodus 17, striking granite would give glory to God for the miracle. In Numbers 20, striking the limestone would give glory to Moses for being a wise reader of the rock. Thus when Moses strikes the rock in Numbers 20 rather than speaking to it, he hears the judgment of God. "Because you did not trust in me enough to honor me as holy in the sight of the Israelites, you will not bring this community into the land I give them" (Numbers 20:12).

THE EASTERN PLATEAU

The final region we will discuss during our visit to the land of milk and honey is the one located immediately east of the Jordan River, a region we will call the eastern plateau. During the time of Joshua, three of the twelve tribes (Reuben, Gad, and one-half of Manasseh) held tribal territory on this side of the Jordan River. The east side of the Jordan River was also home to nations that interacted frequently with God's Old Testament people: the Ammonites, Moabites, and Edomites. During the New Testament, Jesus occasionally ventured to the east side of the Jordan during His ministry on earth. At this time, the land east of the Jordan was under the controlling hand of Rome. It divided that territory into subdistricts like Gaulanitis, Tranconitis, the Decapolis, and Perea.

While the number of biblical events occurring east of the Jordan River is fewer than those recorded to the west, greater geographical awareness of the eastern plateau will lead us to a deeper appreciation of the stories that are set there. For example, Moses and the Israelites spent time on the east side of the Jordan River. Although Moses was disqualified from leading the Israelites into the Promised Land, he was still given the chance to see the land from a distance. The viewing platform was Mount Nebo, a mountain that lies northeast of the Dead Sea. Later, King David was successful in expanding his kingdom to include the land east of the Jordan River, which extended his holdings as far as the Syrian Desert. Both he and his son, Solomon, benefited from the natural resources offered by

Ammon, Moab, and Edom. Jesus Himself traveled across the Sea of Galilee to the Decapolis where He healed a man vexed by demonic possession. Because of these stories and others like them, we will now make a brief visit to the eastern plateau.

Geography

The entire eastern plateau stretches for 250 miles from the base of Mount Hermon in the north to the Gulf of Eilat in the south. The width of this plateau varies from 70 miles to 20 miles due to the intrusion and retreat of Syrian Desert sand on its eastern border. This territory is wider where the terrain rises and blocks the intrusion of the desert sand, and it is narrower where the terrain of the eastern plateau opens itself to the desert sand.

When viewed from the western side of the Jordan River, the eastern plateau does not look like a plateau at all but a towering mountain wall that rises abruptly from the Jordan rift valley. (See photo 26.) However, this mountain-like appearance is only evident on the far western side of the region. After a strenuous hike up the steep face of the western slope, the traveler hiking east through the region will find that the mountains level and become a plateau. This high tableland stretches for miles but is interrupted by several deeply incised canyons that run from west to east. During the biblical period, these canyons not only formed a barrier to north-south traffic but also formed political boundaries.[1] From north to south, the major canyons are associated with the Yarmuk River, the Jabbok River, the Arnon River, and the Zered River.

With the exception of the far north, where previous volcanic activity has left its mark on the land, the surface area of the eastern plateau is composed mainly of Cenomanian and Senonian limestone with Nubian sandstone beneath. Erosion of the upper limestone layers in the south means that the red sandstone becomes more evident there.[2] This erosion is induced by greater rainfall in the area. Because the terrain east of the Jordan River is higher than the terrain to the west of the Jordan River, uplifted air masses deposit significant rains on the upwind side of the eastern plateau. That means that the canyons house rivers that drain the eastern portions of the plateau to the Jordan rift valley.

BASHAN

We will now take a closer look at each of the major sub-regions of the eastern plateau beginning in the north with Bashan. The region of Bashan extends 55 miles from the base of Mount Hermon to the foothills of Gilead, and so lies mainly north of the Yarmuk River. It stretches east and west for 70 miles between the Jordan rift valley and the Syrian Desert. The greater width of the region is attributable to the rising terrain to the east. A range of snow-capped mountains rising to 5,000 feet above sea level (called Mount Hauran or Jebel Druze) block intrusion of the Syrian Desert sand into this area. As we move from north to south through Bashan, changes in geography are again very apparent and so are discussed separately below.

Upper Bashan

Upper Bashan lies to the northwest of Mount Hauran and is called the Leja or Traconitis. Its volcanic history has led geographers to describe this area as both a "basaltic desert"[3] and a "petrified ocean."[4] Both names fit well, for the Leja is an undulating sea of lava. Its irregular ridges of shiny black rock rise up to 40 feet, and create small basins that are virtually devoid of soil. Given this topographical and geologic reality, the Leja favors neither agriculture nor travel, but functions as a refuge for bandits and rebels. This is how it gets its Arabic name Leja, which means "refuge." In the New Testament era, this region is assigned to Herod's son Philip and receives the name Traconitis, the "torn land."

Lower Bashan

By contrast, the region of Lower Bashan (New Testament Gaulanitis) is a high plateau broken by the occasional extinct volcanic cone.[5] The rain-bearing winds are able to penetrate much more deeply into this region and provide it with more significant rainfall because the hills of Lower Galilee demand less water from the eastward marching air masses, and because the terrain of Bashan rises gently from west to east.[6] With up to 40 inches of precipitation falling on fertile volcanic soil, this land produces a significant harvest.[7] When George Smith visited the region, he noted that the threshing floors of Bashan were unique because they were regularly filled with 2 to 3 feet of sheaves,[8] which gave credence to the claim that

Bashan is the granary of ancient Israel.[9] When too many basaltic boulders prevented plowing, animals were grazed on the rich pastures. The bulls of Bashan that grew strong on the nutrients from those pastures are noted by biblical authors in Psalm 22:12 and Ezekiel 39:18. When Amos calls the wives of Samaria's elite citizens "cows of Bashan," he is not making reference to their appearance but to the gaudy wealth they had collected at the expense of the poor (Amos 4:1). Apart from agriculture and livestock, the higher elevations of Bashan also produced important forest products. Zechariah refers to the oak trees of Bashan in the same breath as he speaks of the magnificent cedars of Lebanon (Zechariah 11:2). Ezekiel further notes that this oak was used by the Phoenicians in order to make oars for their boats (Ezekiel 27:6). Given the rich natural resources of this land, it is not surprising that the Israelites had to fight in order to obtain it when they arrived in the region. Moses summarizes the battle Joshua fought against King Og of Bashan for control of this area in Numbers 21:33–35.

GILEAD

Immediately south of Bashan lies the region of Gilead. The foothills of Gilead make an appearance about 18 miles south of the Yarmuk River. From there, Gilead stretches southward for approximately 55 miles and terminates just north of the Dead Sea. As there is no mountain chain to protect Gilead from the intrusion of the desert sands on its eastern boundary, it is much narrower than Bashan and achieves a width of just 25 to 30 miles.

Topography and Geology

South of the Yarmuk River, the volcanic elements associated with Bashan quickly disappear and leave the heartland of Gilead to mirror the landscape and vegetation of the mountains lying west of the Jordan River.[10] The heartland of Gilead consists of an uplifted dome of Cenomanian limestone[11] with just a few places where the Nubian sandstone is exposed in the Jabbok River canyon.[12] These high and rugged mountains reach altitudes of over 4,000 feet above sea level in the north and are cut everywhere by narrow valleys. But once we travel south of the Jabbok River, the landscape changes again. The forested ridges of northern Gilead give way to an extensive plateau that extends beyond the borders of Gilead into Moab.[13]

Natural Resources

The rising terrain of Gilead snatches water from the atmosphere and delivers between 28 and 32 inches of annual precipitation to the surface.[14] This water mixes with the soil to generate greenery both in the mountains and on the plateau. In particular, the mountain ridges of Gilead were heavily forested in antiquity. These forests remained in place well into the nineteenth century, for Smith observed that one could walk all day in the shade of those forests when traveling through the region.[15] In addition to the shade, those forests also provided a product that the biblical authors call the balm of Gilead. A caravan of Ishmaelite traders was carrying this product to Egypt when they encountered Joseph's brothers who were anxious to sell Joseph as a slave (Genesis 37:25). While the exact nature of this product is not known, it appears to be a form of tree sap that was highly regarded for its medicinal purposes (Jeremiah 8:22; 46:11).

The plentiful rains of Gilead also found their way to the agricultural fields and pastures of the plateau where they met with fertile terra rossa soil. This region becomes the only place in the area east of the Jordan River that it is possible to grow grain, grapes, and olives together.[16] The rich vegetation that grows naturally here also makes it a very desirable location for pasturing livestock. The tribes of both Reuben and Gad found this quality of Gilead so attractive that they asked Moses if they could locate themselves in this region (Numbers 32:1–5) rather than in the land on the west side of the Jordan River.

Biblical History

During the Old Testament, the Ammonites frequently controlled the eastern side of Gilead and exerted their influence from their capital at Rabbah (now Amman, the capital of Jordan). This city, located on the fringe of the desert, was able to thrive due to the trade that passed through on the nearby King's Highway.[17] As David began to expand the influence of his kingdom, Rabbah became an important target because it controlled trade on the King's Highway. Thus it is not surprising that David sent his army to attack this city. What is surprising is that he stayed home, leading to his sin with Bathsheba (2 Samuel 11:1). The rich and impressive city would fall to David but eventually regained its autonomy. Ezekiel forecasted that this renewed city would become a pastureland because they celebrated on the day Israel was taken into exile by Babylon (Ezekiel 25:5). Another city of Gilead that finds its way onto the pages of our Bible is the city of Jabesh Gilead. It was attacked by Nahash the Ammonite shortly after Saul had been identified as Israel's first king. His rescue of Jabesh Gilead was the battle that led the people to confirm him as their king (1 Samuel 11). This act of devotion to Jabesh Gilead would later be repaid after the death of Saul. When the Philistines took his body and hung it on the wall at Beth Shan, soldiers from Jabesh Gilead went to Beth Shan to get Saul's remains and bury them near their city (1 Samuel 31:11–13).

During the time of the New Testament, most cities of the Roman Decapolis were located in the region of Gilead. The Decapolis cities included: Damascus, Philadelphia, Raphana, Scythopolis (Beth Shan), Gadara, Hippos, Dion, Pella, Galasa, and Canatha. Although many of these cities were established by Greek-speaking citizens before Roman domination of the region, they were used by the Romans to spread Greco-Roman culture and ideology as well as to administer and control the territory around them. Planning for such cities included the construction of hippodromes, theaters, forums, cardos, and temples.

Several of these Decapolis cities find their way into the pages of the New Testament either by allusion or formal reference. For example, the city of Hippos stood high above the eastern shore of the Sea of Galilee. Anyone living on the west side of the lake would easily see its lights at night. Jesus may well be alluding to the lights from that city when instructing His followers during the Sermon on the Mount. In the sermon, when He spoke about the powerful influence that His followers could have on the world, He said, "You are the light of the world. A city on a hill cannot be hidden" (Matthew 5:14).

Because of the strong pagan culture associated with these cities, conservative Jews of Jesus' time viewed these cities as horrid places. They were in so many ways, "the other side" (Mark 4:35). But Jesus' loving ministry extended even to those who raised pigs on "the other side." He met a demon-possessed man who was living naked in a cemetery (Mark 5:1–20). After removing a legion of demons from him, this unnamed man becomes the missionary who brings the message of the Gospel to the Decapolis cities (Mark 5:20). This ministry was richly blessed by the Holy Spirit. When Jesus returned to the Decapolis, thousands of people turned out to hear His message (Mark 7:31–8:13).

Moab

South of Gilead is the region that we will call Moab. It extends approximately 55 miles from the northern reaches of the Dead Sea southward to the Arnon River gorge. Its width varies between 20 and 25 miles. The heart of the plateau is composed of Cenomanian limestone but boasts beautiful red Nubian sandstone cliffs along the shore of the Dead Sea. The eastern portions of the plateau are characterized by increasing amounts of Senonian chalk.[18] The region is split by the impressive Arnon River gorge that rivals the Grand Canyon in terms of beauty and grandeur. This canyon narrows from nearly 3 miles at the rim to only 40 yards at the riverbed with walls that exceed 2,300 feet.[19] This gorge divides the region into two segments. The biblical writers refer to the northern segment as the Mishor and the southern segment as Moab proper (though the Moabites frequently controlled both sections).

The Mishor

The Mishor is a rolling tableland undulating between 2,000 and 2,400 feet above sea level north of the Arnon River. The land in this region is lower in elevation and less dissected than the areas south of the Arnon River. The lower elevations mean that the area will receive less precipitation than the rising terrain to the south. Here the seasonal rainfall averages only about 10 inches annually.[20]

Heartland of Moab

South of the Arnon River is where we find the heartland of Moab. In this region, the plateau rises to over 4,000 feet in elevation and becomes more dissected by tributaries and small canyons.[21] As the mountains of Moab are higher than those of Judah, rain that cannot be extracted from the atmosphere over Judah may be extracted over Moab. This means that the western rim of the plateau receives sufficient rainfall to grow grain. Naomi and her family were aware of this geographical reality. When a famine gripped the fields around Bethlehem, the rainfall in Moab permitted a grain harvest (Ruth 1:1). Thus Naomi and her family traveled from the Judean Highlands to Moab during the time of famine. This opens the door for a young Moabite woman named Ruth to travel back to Bethlehem and begin a family that eventually gives birth to David (Ruth 4:21).

While grain may be harvested on the western fringes of Moab, most of the plateau is too dry for predictable agriculture. This makes Moab a land that is best known for its pastoral products. During the time of Israel's King Joram, King Mesha of Moab paid an annual tribute of 100,000 lambs and with the wool of 100,000 rams (2 Kings 3:4). Revenue from trade was also part of the privilege of controlling Moab. Two branches of the King's Highway passed through this region. One branch traversed the watershed of the plateau and the other traveled along the desert fringes to the east.[22] Both routes carried goods between the Red Sea and Damascus. But both also had their drawbacks. Those traveling on the eastern route had to contend with desert raiders, while those traveling the watershed line had to contend with crossing the Arnon River gorge.

Moses notes in Genesis 19:36–39 that the Moabites were related to Lot. But that family relationship did not guarantee friendly relations between Moab and Israel. As the Israelites camped on the Plains of Moab opposite Jericho preparing for war, they waited for the divine command to cross the Jordan River. King Balak of Moab felt threatened by their presence so he summoned a man named Balaam to put a curse on the Israelites. But when it was time for Balaam to curse them, the Lord only allowed him to bless them (Numbers 22–24). That blessing was tarnished as the men of Israel began to engage in sexually inappropriate behavior with Moabite women linked to Baal worship. This sin resulted in a plague that took 24,000 lives (Numbers 25:1–18). Later, Moses himself would use a portion of Moab as the viewing platform from which he would get his one and only view of the Promised Land. As Moses stood upon 2,631-foot Mount Nebo located 12 miles east Jericho, he had a commanding view of the Lower Jordan River Valley, the Dead Sea, and the Judean Highlands (Deuteronomy 34). Once the Israelites had established themselves in the land, the residents of Moab frequently wrestled with Israel for control of the Mishor. The animosity led to divine judgment against Moab announced by prophets like Amos (Amos 2:1–3).

EDOM

Topography and Geology

South of Moab we encounter the land of Edom. The Mountains of Edom are the mountains that rise immediately above and to the east of the Arabah. This region extends 110 miles from the Zered River to the Gulf of Eilat. The ridge that runs along the spine of that mountain chain is approximately 15 miles in width, which is where the people of Edom live. The mountains themselves are composed of a variety of materials. Typically, the western face of the ridge boasts the orange, red, yellow, and violet hues of Nubian sandstone.[23] These colors are particularly vibrant as the sun strikes them early in the morning. This undoubtedly explains the Hebrew name "Edom," which alludes to the red color of the cliffs. A visit to the Nabatean capital at Petra shows how beautifully this sandstone can be shaped and sculpted. As we move eastward where the plateau meets the desert, the sandstone gives way to Cenomanian limestone and finally Senonian chalk.[24] Observing Edom from the Arabah, we are struck by the dominating height of the mountains rising over 5,600 feet above us. We can fully appreciate why the prophet Jeremiah referred to the residents of Edom as those who made their nests with the eagles (Jeremiah 49:16).

Natural Resources

Because the terrain of Edom lies so far above the terrain of the Negev, the heights of Edom tap the moisture-laden air masses moving off the Mediterranean Sea. The northern portions of Edom receive from 16 to 20 inches of annual precipitation, which make agriculture possible. But the farther south you go, the less rain is available. The amount of rain that falls on the southern end of Edom totals just over 2 inches per year.[25] The rainfall in the north provided nutrition for the scrub forests that grew in the mountains southeast of the Dead Sea. From a distance, the mountains looked as if they were hairy. So the Israelites named them the Mountains of Seir (Genesis 36:9), which means "hairy mountains." Beneath the surface and within the sandstone, miners mined copper ore that was smelted at places like Punom and Timnah by using wood from those same forests.[26]

Culture

In most respects, the mountains defined the culture of those living there. The topography of those mountains prevented large-scale agricultural operations but permitted nomadic herding, though to a lesser extent than was common in Moab. The one major source of revenue for the residents of Moab, therefore, was in their ability to control and tax the merchants using the trade routes between the Gulf of Aqaba, the Mediterranean Sea, and Damascus. Trade goods moving along the King's Highway from Ezion Geber might move directly northward to Damascus or move down one of the key passes, the Wadi Fidan from Punom or the Wadi Musa at Petra.[27] In either case, the terrain limited the choice in travel routes and so allowed the residents of Edom to tax the goods moving on this roadway. The high mountains also afforded the Edomites a natural stronghold that was very difficult to penetrate, and led the Edomites to have a reputation for fierce independence.[28]

Biblical History

This independent spirit becomes evident in the exchange between Israel and Edom recorded by Moses in Numbers 20. Israel's time in the Wilderness of Zin was complete and so they began to move in the direction of the Promised Land. They apparently crossed the Arabah and asked the Edomites for permission to use a mountain pass (possibly at Punom) to gain access to the King's Highway. The Israelite correspondence was careful to mention that they would not damage their natural resources en route, but only wanted to travel via the King's Highway through their land (Numbers 20:14–20). By all counts, the number of soldiers that Edom could place in the field was far less than the number of soldiers that Israel could place in the field. Yet when the Edomites declined Israel permission, Israel did not fight but made a detour of 175 miles around Edom. Undoubtedly, the thought of having to fight their way up the mountain passes, even against a smaller defensive force, played a role in their decision (Numbers 21:4).

Despite the fact that both peoples were related to one another through brothers (Israel via Jacob and Edom via Esau), subsequent relations between Edom and Israel were sometimes cordial and supportive, and other times hostile and hateful. Edom came under the sway of David and Solomon (2 Samuel 8:14), but frequently rebelled against Israel and Judah in the years that followed (2 Kings 3 and 8:20). When the Babylonians took the Israelites into exile, the Edomites gloated, celebrated, and even looted God's people (Psalm 137:7). That brought about the formal declaration of divine judgment announced by Obadiah. Notice how he employs the geography of Edom during the introduction to the message of judgment. "The pride of your heart has deceived you, you who live in the clefts of the rocks and make your home on the heights, you who say to yourself, 'Who can bring me down to the ground?' Though you soar like the eagle and make your nest among the stars, from there I will bring you down, declares the LORD" (Obadiah 1:3–4).

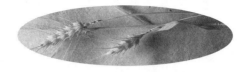

13

HYDROLOGY AND CLIMATE

The most fundamental, physical need that human beings face is the need for fresh water. And if there is one thing that the Promised Land has in very short supply, it is fresh water. Because this life-giving liquid is nearly absent, it is arguably the geographical factor that has the greatest impact on the way people live and think in this land. The average resident of ancient Israel would spend a considerable portion of the week discovering, maintaining, and defending a source of fresh water. Given that fact, it is not surprising that water is mentioned with some frequency by the biblical authors in both literal and figurative contexts. For example, water is so critical to the life of the Promised Land that the longing for water becomes a symbol of the longing for God. "As the deer pants for streams of water, so my soul pants for you, O God. My soul thirsts for God, for the living God" (Psalm 42:1–2). When the thirsty Jesus stands before a well in Sychar, He speaks to a Samaritan woman about a special kind of water, the Good News, that removes thirst forever. "Everyone who drinks this water will be thirsty again, but whoever drinks the water I give him will never thirst. Indeed, the water I give him will become in him a spring of water welling up to eternal life" (John 4:13–14).

The goal of this chapter is to investigate the water and the weather in Israel. We will see how very rare and precious fresh water is before we speak about the potential sources of the water in Israel, and the ways that water was collected for personal use. Closely linked to water is the weather. Chances are good that you live in a part of the world where the weather is very different than it is in Israel. In this chapter, we will also discuss the differences in the weather of Israel's two seasons and see how those climatic differences changed the way people lived and worked. The weather patterns often affected the Promised Land, causing severe droughts that definitely would have caused the Israelites to leave the Promised Land. Consequently, we will also discuss the causes, nature, and realities of drought during the biblical period.

A Shortage of Fresh Water

Those who lived in ancient Israel lived a life that was driven and defined by water. In comparison with most other settled areas of the world, Israel is a land that is clearly destitute when it comes to fresh water. That becomes glaringly clear in the following statistics. The minimum amount of water required to maintain a comfortable life is estimated to be 1,000 cubic meters per capita.[1] In 1990, within the United States, each resident had 10,000 cubic meters of water available to him or her. That means that when I think of fresh water potential, I think of having 2.6 million gallons of water available for my personal use. By contrast in that same year, Egypt had 1,100 cubic meters per capita and Israel had a mere 460 cubic meters of water per resident.[2] This is clearly the most significant cultural gap between the biblical reader in the United States and the biblical writer of ancient Israel. My perception of fresh water availability is more than 20 times greater than that of the person living in the modern state of Israel. We can rest assured that the residents of ancient Israel had even less water available to them than the modern residents.

Precipitation-based Hydrology

Many regions within the Fertile Crescent get their water from perennially flowing rivers and freshwater lakes. For example, the residents of ancient Egypt enjoyed a river-based hydrology. Although it did not rain often on the Nile Delta, it did rain in those portions of central Africa that produce the Nile River. This means that the Egyptians living along the river could obtain their water directly from the river, while at the same time redirecting the flow of the Nile to their agricultural fields via irrigation canals. But what was the norm in Egypt was the exception within ancient Israel. The Promised Land does have one freshwater lake and one significant river, but neither is capable of providing enough fresh water for very many residents. The Sea of Galilee is the largest freshwater lake in Israel, but its elevation of 700 feet below sea level makes it impossible for the ancient residents of Israel to transport that water any great distance. Gravity limits this resource to those living in the immediate vicinity of the shoreline. There are a variety of watercourses in Israel, but most of them flow for only a short period of time after it rains.[3] By contrast, the largest river in Israel, the Jordan River, flows regularly, but like the Sea of Galilee, it is at too low in elevation and becomes much too chemical in its southern stretches to be of much value.

Because freshwater lakes and rivers supply a limited amount of water for the citizens of the Promised Land, their primary source of fresh water is the rain that falls from the sky during the winter season. By definition, Israel has a precipitation-based hydrology. As the Israelites were preparing to enter the Promised Land, God made this point very clear to them.

> The land you are entering to take over is not like the land of Egypt, from which you have come, where you planted your seed and irrigated it by foot as in a vegetable garden. But the land you are crossing the Jordan to take possession of is a land of mountains and valleys that drinks rain from heaven (Deuteronomy 11:10–11).

In other words, there would be water for drinking and cooking, for fields and vineyards, for sheep and goats only when it rained. This makes the coming of rain something to be celebrated rather than mourned. Within the ancient Israelite culture you do not find rhymes like, "Rain, rain, go away. Come again another day." And no ancient weather forecaster would lament the possibility of rain on the weekend, because rain is a cause for celebration and hope.

THE UNEQUAL DISTRIBUTION OF RAIN

But not everyone gets to celebrate all of the time or to the same degree because differences in season and location mean that rainfall totals differ significantly from time to time and from place to place. First, the amount of precipitation varies by the season. As we shall see in the discussion of climate below, Israel experiences a season of rain and a season of drought. From November to February, 70 percent of the precipitation received during the year will fall to the ground. By contrast in the months of June through August, there will be no rain.[4] This, of course, has a significant impact on the land. Would you believe that Jerusalem and London receive the same amount of annual precipitation (22 inches)? It is true, but the difference lies in the fact that Jerusalem receives most of that rain in 50 days while London receives it over 300 days.

Second, the amount of precipitation also varies by region. In general, rainfall in Israel diminishes when moving from north to south and from west to east. Typically, the farther north you are in the country, the more rain you will have. For example, in the same year that Mount Hermon receives 60 inches of precipitation, the city of Eilat at the head of the Red Sea might receive only .5 inches of rain. This is because the track of the low pressure areas bring rain from the Mediterranean Sea and across northern Israel more directly.[5] Rainfall also tends to favor the upwind western slopes. The western slopes of rising terrain will typically be wetter than the eastern slopes because the moist air masses are lifted upslope by the prevailing westerly winds. This causes the air masses to cool and disgorge most of their moisture on the upwind slopes while creating a rainfall shadow on the eastern slopes.

But the rainfall picture is much more complex than that. Runoff and evaporation also play a role in the effective rainfall totals because not all of the rain that falls on the ground is absorbed. Approximately 5–15 percent of the rainfall total is lost to runoff while another 70 percent is lost to evaporation.[6] The amount of that evaporation varies with compass orientation. The northern slopes receive less direct sunlight and experience less evaporation than the southern slopes, so they tend to be wetter and greener. Ultimately, the lower the elevation, the farther south and the farther you are from the sea, the less rain you are likely to receive.[7]

WATER ACQUISITION

To live in Israel is to live with the reality that rain controls the lifestyle. Thus the residents of ancient Israel would have spent a significant part of their week discussing ways of obtaining fresh water. Today, technology allows water to be accessed and moved in ways that were not available to the ancient people. For example, the modern state of Israel has dammed up the flow of water from the Sea of Galilee into the Lower Jordan River. That makes the lake basin a reservoir for collecting water that is eventually pumped around the country. High tech drilling has also enabled the modern state to acquire water from deep-water aquifers. Those two sources provide modern residents of this land with most of their water. Of course, the ancient people's ability to access and move water was much more limited. So instead, we see biblical characters going to places like springs, wells, and cisterns for water.

Springs, Wells, and Cisterns

The spring was the most desirable way to obtain water in ancient Israel. Springs break out throughout the land where the water table and terrain lie at the same elevation.[8] But theses springs are not evenly or frequently distributed throughout the country, so the residents of the land would also dig wells. Instead of looking for a place where the water table and terrain existed at the same elevation, people would have to find a place to dig down to the water table. The most desirable place to dig a well is where the least amount of soil needs to be moved, thus wells are often found on the valley floors and in wadi beds.[9] Once the location was picked, the water seeker would excavate a circular hole 1.5 to 2 meters in diameter that would be lined with fieldstone to prevent the well's walls from collapsing.[10] When domestic animals were to be watered, the builder would also construct troughs near the well to limit the distance that water was carried for those animals.[11]

If the residents of this land were to rely only upon springs and wells, the livable space would be very small. But the cistern made it possible for settlements to develop where springs did not exist and where wells were not practical. A cistern is a water collection and storage chamber that is carved into the ground. The containers vary in size depending on whether they were serving a larger town or a single residence. For example, the well at ancient Arad was nearly 53 feet deep and had a capacity of 66,000 gallons of water.[12] But whether for a town or residence, the cisterns shared many characteristics. An underground area is excavated in the shape of a bell or bottle and then sealed with lime plaster to limit the amount of water that would seep out of it. The plaster that sealed the cistern required annual repair and maintenance to keep the cistern watertight.[13] Because rainwater would be used to resupply the cistern, channels were often cut to redirect runoff water to this supply basin. Because that runoff water would also carry undesirable particles with it, settling basins were often included in this channel system to slow the speed of the water and allow particulate matter to settle out. The water would then flow into the cistern through a very narrow neck that would further limit surface contamination.[14] The design of such a cistern helps us understand why the youthful Joseph was unable to get himself out of the dry cistern into which his brothers lowered him (Genesis 37:23–24). Such cisterns also would typically have a cover. When removed, the cover would allow access to the water; when replaced, the cover prevented sunlight from reaching the water, slowing the growth of algae.[15] While such cisterns were not limited to Israelite culture, they are critical to the establishment of Israel in the Promised Land. The cistern allowed the Israelites to spread out and live throughout the hill country without having to cluster around springs and wells.[16]

Dams, Channels, Tunnels, and Aqueducts

The residents of ancient Israel also looked for ways to capture and redirect surface water that was making its way toward the Dead Sea or the Mediterranean Sea. For example, the residents of Qumran had a great need for water due both to the personal and ceremonial function of water among them. They constructed their settlement near a place where surface water would rush out of the Judean Wilderness toward the Dead Sea. By constructing a dam to block the flow of water to the sea, the residents of Qumran were able to redirect that water by channels and decantation pools to large cisterns in their complex.[17]

The Nabateans also invested a considerable amount of time in creating a water resource for their agriculture fields in the marginal southern desert. After identifying a small watershed area in the hills, they would carefully recraft the surface to direct the water flow into their fields. Small stone mounds, once thought to be ancient grape trellises, were more likely stone piles formed when fieldstones were removed from the targeted area to increase the water flow towards the channels. Those channels directed water off the slopes to terraced watercourses. The speed of the water was slowed by the terraces so that more water was absorbed by the agriculture fields.[18]

When one had the financial resources, water could be transported over short or long distances using tunnels, channels, and aqueducts. For example, tunnels were used in cities like Hazor, Megiddo, and Jerusalem. The tunnels transported water hundreds of feet from springs outside the city walls to people living within the city walls. This was particularly important during a time of siege. Perhaps the best known tunnel of this nature is Hezekiah's Tunnel located in Jerusalem. After King Hezekiah declared a religious reformation that also entailed a dissolution of the treaty with Assyria, he knew that the Assyrians would be back to reclaim Jerusalem. He prepared the city of Jerusalem for siege by expanding the walled-in area of the city, and by building a tunnel that brought water from the Gihon Spring outside the wall in the Kidron Valley, to the Siloam Pool inside the city wall (2 Kings 20:20 and 2 Chronicles 32:30). This meant tunneling more than 1/3 of a mile underground to connect a spring that could produce up to 316,000 gallons of water per day for the residents of Jerusalem.[19]

As magnificent as this feat was, it did not top the efforts of King Herod the Great. The water demands of his Jerusalem exceeded any local sources, so he constructed a system that carried water from the hill country south of Jerusalem over 15 miles to the city.[20] A similar system supplied water to his city of Caesarea Philippi. Water was brought from the southern slopes of Mount Carmel to this city by way of a system of channels and raised aqueducts that stretched over 13 miles.[21]

Rain and Theology

As you can plainly see, rain and obtaining water dominated the thinking and lifestyle of those living in this land. It also strongly influenced their theology. By contrast to the neighboring lands of Egypt and Mesopotamia, where the chief deity in the heathen pantheon was the sun God (Amun-Re in Egypt and Markduk in Babylon), the primary deity among the Canaanites was Baal.[22] Baal was the deity who provided the rain that made the crops grow and filled the cisterns.[23] The Canaanites believed that they could influence and manipulate their deities by specific acts and rituals and ultimately control the circumstances in their own lives. Because they believed that rainfall was the semen of Baal, they thought they could produce rain by stimulating him sexually. This was done via a religious system that included temple prostitution and pornographic images both designed to arouse Baal and bring rain to the land.[24]

God knew that He was bringing His chosen people to a land that was contaminated by this kind of theology, so He went out of His way to help them fend off the temptation of this Canaanite thinking. Even before the Israelites crossed the Jordan River with Joshua, God made it clear that the Promised Land was a land that relied upon the rain to survive, and that He and He alone was the author of that rainfall.

> The land you are crossing the Jordan to take possession of is a land of mountains and valleys that drinks rain from heaven. It is a land the LORD your God cares for; the eyes of the LORD your God are continually on it from the beginning of the year to its end. So if you faithfully obey the commands I am giving you today . . . then I will send rain on your land in its season, both autumn and spring rains, so that you may gather in your grain, new wine and oil. (Deuteronomy 11:11–14)

Apparently the Israelites learned to farm and worship Baal at the same time. This tutoring was necessary because their experience in the previous centuries was associated with the river-based hydrology of Egypt. When they arrived in the Promised Land, their Canaanite neighbors not only taught them about the planting cycles associated with a rain-based hydrology but also taught the Israelites to worship Baal. Thus, despite preliminary instructions and the warnings from the Lord, the Israelites regularly assimilated both the thinking and practices of Baal worship into their lives.

The sin of Baal worship is regularly reported by the biblical authors throughout the rest of the Old Testament, for it represented a fundamental misunderstanding of Israel's relationship to God. He made it abundantly clear to them that He was the source of rain. (See, for example, Deuteronomy 11:10–15; Job 5:10 and 36:27–28; Psalm 135:7 and 147:8; Isaiah 30:23–26; Zechariah 10:1.) God also made it clear that when they honored Him with the lifestyle He had designed for them, rain would fall. "If you follow my decrees and are careful to obey my commands, I will send you rain in its season" (Leviticus 26:3–4). Failure to honor God with this lifestyle would result in drought (1 Kings 8:35–36; 17:1; Haggai 1:10–11). Thus rain became a critical part of the theology of Israel. It is the cyclic return to Baal worship that causes the cycle of blessing and pain we read in the book of Judges. And it is the assimilation of Baal worship that brings about the Assyrian and Babylonian exiles (1 Kings 17:7–23).

WEATHER

Water defines the Israelite lifestyle more than any other factor, but it is also very closely associated with the weather and climate of this land. Because there are no formal climatic records of the Promised Land before the modern era, what we know about the climate of ancient Israel depends heavily upon extrapolation from modern data. Where the Bible and other ancient records from the biblical period include information about the weather, it is largely in harmony with the modern climatic data. It is presumed that this land, lying between 29 and 33 degrees north latitude, has approximately the same sub-tropical climate today as it had in the biblical period. This means that the year in Israel consists basically of two seasons—a rainy winter and a dry summer.[25]

Of course, that does not mean that the entire country experiences the same kind of weather on any given day. North-south location in this land, position with relationship to the desert and the sea, and the presence or absence of rising terrain all play a role in creating a very diverse fabric of microclimates. For example, though Jerusalem and Jericho lie only 15 miles apart, they can experience very different weather within the same hour. The author has experienced sunny and 75 degrees at Jericho before experiencing 45 degrees and rain in Jerusalem just thirty minutes later. In the earlier chapters, we made an effort to call attention to the local nuances of weather that impacted the regions under discussion. Here, we will enjoy a more general look at the climate of Israel attending to the differences between summer, winter, and transitional seasons.

Summer

The summer season in Israel lasts from mid-June through mid-September. The most striking aspect about this summer season is its monotony. Each day is the same with high humidity, cloudless skies, warm temperatures, southwesterly winds, and no rain. As the jet stream migrates to the north during these months, high pressure settles in over the region. Such high pressure areas are characterized by descending air molecules that compress the atmosphere at lower elevations, create warm temperatures near the surface, and very light winds.[26] As the seasonal high makes its presence felt over the eastern Mediterranean, the moisture from the sea is brought up into the atmosphere, but not lifted above the dew point due to the descending air associated with the high pressure area. So while the humidity may be high, no clouds or rain form. The atmosphere is not expected to change all summer because the jet stream carries migrating low pressure areas to the north. This makes Israel one of the sunniest countries in the world.[27]

That constant summer sun can actually do damage to the soil. In some areas, the drying of the soil becomes so intense that water is drawn up and out of the soil by capillary action. The result of this extraction is that natural salts are brought to the soil's surface and diminish its surface fertility.[28] The heat can also sap the energy of animals and humans alike (Psalm 32:4), making it necessary to rest during the warmest parts of the day (Genesis 18:1) so as to avoid the threat of both fatigue and dehydration (Psalm 121:6).

Summertime in Israel is also affected by a local low pressure area that forms over the island of Cyprus due to the sun baking its central plain. This minor low does not migrate, but does cause the light southwesterly winds to blow across the region and push the humidity further inland. Of course, the humid air makes the temperature feel even warmer. The summer temperature in Jerusalem averages 86 degrees during the day and 64 degrees during the night.[29] Temperatures on the coast are predictably several degrees cooler than in the interior of the country. The cooler air is due to the sea breeze that develops each day about 9 a.m. When the sun rises in the sky, the air over the land warms more quickly than the air over the sea. As the warm air over the land rises, the cooler air above the sea rushes in to replace it, creating a sea breeze. This refreshing breeze reaches Jerusalem around 1:00 p.m., offers some relief from the summer heat, and presents the farmers in the highlands with a predictable wind to winnow their harvested grain.[30]

Under such sunny conditions, shade becomes a very critical resource. Trees are at a premium, so rock outcroppings and ridges provide a more likely opportunity for shade. Shepherds moving their animals to new pastures during the summer months will often pick a route that will permit the shadow of a ridge to keep them cool during the warmest part of the day.[31] The author himself has seen a Bedouin camp built completely around a rock outcropping. As the shadow of the rock moves during the day, so do the family's activities in order to stay out of the direct sun. This is the picture Isaiah had in mind when he spoke about the "shadow of a great rock in a thirsty land" (Isaiah 32:2). And this undoubtedly is the image of comfort David had in view when he spoke of the Lord being his rock of consolation (Psalm 18:2).

Dew is also critical for sustaining life at a time when the sky has neither rain nor clouds in it. During the day, moisture-laden air is driven inland by the wind. When evening comes, the atmosphere is granted relief from the direct rays of the sun; when it cools, it reduces the ability of that air to carry moisture. The cooling air is anxious to disgorge its moisture on any surface below the dew point. The result is that Israel has between 150 and 250 dew nights per year with the greater number of nights occurring on Mount Carmel and in the Negev.[32] During his travels in the land, George Smith observed that during many summer mornings, the ground was drenched with moisture as if there had been a heavy rain.[33] This moisture is critical to the survival of many plants. While the grain crops have been harvested by the middle of the summer, other crops like olives, grapes, and figs are ripening. This dew can provide up to 25 percent of the moisture that plants like these need to survive through the drought of summer.[34]

This dewfall becomes part of the literature of Israel through the inspired writers. When Zechariah speaks of the blessings that Israel will enjoy upon returning to the Promised Land after their time in exile, he says, "The seed will grow well, the vine will yield its fruit, the ground will produce its crops, and the heavens will drop their dew" (Zechariah 8:12). While dew may be an almost unnoticed part of your life, it was integral to survival in Israel. It was so important to survival that the Lord compares His very presence in Israel to the dew. "I will be like the dew to Israel; he will blossom like a lily" (Hosea 14:5).

As we have already seen, the summer season favors certain types of activities while it discourages others. The early summer season is the time for harvesting the grain crops. Together with that harvest, Old Testament believers celebrated the Lord's provision during the Feast of Weeks. This was also the time of the year when the roadways would be in the best possible condition for travel. That means that families, merchants, and armies would use the summer months to travel for pleasure or business. Once the grain was harvested and the roadways dried out, late spring or early summer was the time when the kings would go off to war (2 Samuel 11:1).

Winter

The winter season brings changes as the atmosphere itself takes on new characteristics. A permanent trough develops across the Mediterranean Sea from west to east.[35] Up to 25 low pressure systems march down this trough each year and take aim at the Promised Land.[36] By contrast to the high pressure that dominates the atmosphere in the summer months, these low pressure areas are made of rising air. They lift the moisture from the sea and propel it up past the dew point so that clouds are formed. The higher the moist air is lifted, the colder the air becomes around it. Eventually, the moist air can no longer hold up against the forces of gravity, and water droplets precipitate from the clouds. When such a low pressure area reaches Israel, the sky becomes cloudy and rain begins to fall. After the passage of the low pressure area, north and northeast winds can drive Siberian air masses into Israel[37] and strike the land with a blast of freezing air and frost.[38] While temperatures are cooler than in the summer months, the winters in Israel are considered mild by most people's standards. The average temperature in Jerusalem drops to 50 degrees in January with many evenings in the upper 30s to lower 40s. Thus the atmosphere dictates that the winter season in Israel will be relatively cold, cloudy, and rainy.

However, when we say that winter is the rainy season, it does not mean that it will rain each and every day. In fact, the rainy season itself has a cycle (Deuteronomy 11:14). The early rains are the rains of October through early November. The occasional precipitation during these months takes the form of showers and thunderstorms that contribute about 11 percent of the total rainfall for the year.[39] These early rains are the planting rains. After the summer sun has baked the agricultural fields for months, these rains are necessary to soften the soil for plowing and planting. The farmers waited patiently for these rains. James saw patient waiting for rain as a metaphor for the way believers wait for the Lord's second coming (James 5:7). When the early rains began, the farmers used a scratch plow to break open the surface of the soil and then broadcast their seed as they walk. A second pass of the plow at right angles covers the grain in anticipation of the middle rains,[40] which fall from December through February. During these months, the land receives 75 percent of the annual rainfall expected.[41] This time of the year, it is typical for one low pressure area to strike the land per week. The average week begins with a very hard rain on the first day, then one or two days of scattered showers before a final day of occasional fine rain. After several such days of clouds and rain, the sun typically shines.[42] The amount of water received during this season of the middle rains is critical because it either makes or breaks the quality of the maturing grain crops. Finally, the latter rains fall during the months of March and April. This rain provides the final 14 percent of the rain for the year and brings the crops to maturity. It again takes the form of scattered showers and thunderstorms.[43]

Rain is the predominant form of precipitation during this season, but it is not the only form. Snow can fall on elevations above 2,500 feet and remain for a few days[44] even accumulating to some depth. Jerusalem gets snow about two days per year that accumulates to an inch or more.[45] The author has been in Jerusalem when it has received over 8 inches of snow in just one night, a storm that effectively shut down the city for two days. Such snowfall is so uncommon that it could be used to mark a unique day such as the one in which Benaiah went into a pit and killed a lion (2 Samuel 23:20). Hail is also mentioned in connection with several biblical stories. This form of precipitation typically forms in the more violent cold front thunderstorms associated with late spring.[46]

The characteristics of the winter season in Israel affected the emotions and the activities of those living in Israel. The early fall was a time of great anticipation. Would the early rains begin in time and be enough to plant grain crop? This expectation became part of the October Feast of Tabernacles. The feast was a time to recall how God led His people through the wilderness to the Promised Land while the people lived in portable shelters. But according to the Mishnah (Sukkah), it also became a time for drawing water from the Pool of Siloam in Jerusalem and pouring it on the ground in anticipation of coming rain. Thus the feast had also become a time when the rainy season was anticipated. When Jesus came to Jerusalem for this festival (John 7), He used this occasion and the expectation of rain to invite people to come to Him for living water. "If anyone is thirsty, let him come to Me and drink. Whoever believes in Me, as the Scripture has said, streams of living water will flow from within him" (John 7:37–38).

Celebration and Famine

When the rain finally came, people celebrated. The rainy season was a time of great joy (Proverbs 16:15) as the land itself was transformed from the drab and desiccated browns of summer to rich patterns of green. In poetic verse, the psalmist surveys the land after rain noting its impact on the streams, grain fields, hillsides, and meadows (Psalm 65:9–13). But that season of joy could become one of troubling sadness if the rains were either late or inadequate. "Years of drought and famine run like a scarlet thread through the history of ancient Palestine."[47] Such famine had a devastating impact on the country. Jeremiah captures the image well when he says, "The nobles send their servants for water; they go to the cisterns but find no water. They return with their jars unfilled; dismayed and despairing, they cover their heads. The ground is cracked because there is no rain in the land; the farmers are dismayed and cover their heads. Even the doe in the field deserts her newborn fawn because there is no grass" (Jeremiah 14:3–5). As food supplies dwindle, the cost rises and hunger ravages the land, first claiming the young and then the weak. The Bible itself speaks of other maladies associated with famine like disease (1 Kings 8:37), pestilence (Deuteronomy 32:24), captivity (Jeremiah 15:2), and the collapse of morality (2 Kings 6:25–29).[48] A particularly severe famine would cause residents of Israel to migrate to places where more rain or a major river would provide the guarantee of water. It is because of a famine that we see Naomi's family migrating to Moab (Ruth 1:1) and the patriarchs moving to Egypt (Genesis 12:10; 26:1–2; and 46:3). The decision to move was not an easy one. God had promised the Israelites that this would be their land and the place on which the Messiah would be revealed. No wonder Jacob needed direct communication from God before he dared set foot outside of Israel (Genesis 46:3).

Transitional Seasons

Between the major seasons of winter and summer, there are a few weeks of transition when one of the worst forms of weather strikes the land; the "hamsin" or the "sharav" winds that come off the desert. These winds are caused by a low pressure area developing over northern Africa and Egypt that brings intense east or southeasterly winds to Israel.[49] Wind speeds can exceed 60 miles per hour and fill the air with a yellow, gritty haze that can last anywhere from three days to one week. During this time, the temperature increases 27 degrees above normal with the humidity dropping to less than 10 percent.[50] William Thomson's experience with this phenomenon created a lasting impression caught in the following description:

> The air becomes loaded with fine dust, which it whirls in rainless clouds hither and thither at its own will; it rushes down every gorge, bending and breaking the trees, and tugging at each individual leaf; it growls round the houses, runs riot with your clothes, and flies away with your hat; nor is their any escape from its impertinence. The eyes inflame, the lips blister, and the moisture of the body evaporates under the ceaseless pertinacity of this persecuting wind; you become languid, nervous, irritable, and despairing.[51]

This east wind wilts the winter vegetation so that it is here one day and gone another. This led the inspired authors to use this image to describe the brevity of life. "As for man, his days are like grass, he flourishes like the flower of the field; the wind blows over it and it is gone, and its place remembers it no more" (Psalm 103:15–16). The east wind also becomes a symbol of judgment. Jeremiah described the coming invasion of the Babylonians as a divinely sponsored "hamsin" that would scorch his disobedient people (Jeremiah 4:11–12).

Water and weather play a powerful role in shaping the culture and communication of those living within the Promised Land. Climate directly controls the rainfall, and rainfall directly controls the availability of drinking water, the agricultural cycle, and one's sense of well-being. Given the critical role that water plays in Israel, we are not surprised to find both direct mention of, and allusion to, water on the pages of our Bibles. And when these inspired authors looked for something precious on earth to which they might compare eternal life, water becomes a consistent choice. "Everyone who drinks this water will be thirsty again, but whoever drinks the water I give him will never thirst. Indeed, the water I give him will become in him a spring of water welling up to eternal life" (John 4:13–14).

14

URBANIZATION

R eaders of God's Word will immediately recognize the names of cities like Jerusalem, Bethlehem, and Hebron, though there are hundreds of cities named in the Bible. Why were the urban centers, both large and small, built where they were? How do we know where those ancient cities and villages were located? When people like Abraham or Peter entered those cities, what did the buildings look like that provided them with shelter? You may be surprised to discover that geography plays an important role in answering each of those questions. In this chapter, we will discuss the geographical realities that caused people to establish communities where they did during the biblical period. We will explore how geography and archaeology team up in order to place biblical cities on our maps. We will also find how geography affected both the design and composition of the homes occupied by biblical characters.

SETTLEMENT FACTORS

When members of the biblical world established a village or city, they did so on the basis of certain geographical factors. Archaeologists call these "settlement factors." While a list of possible settlement factors could contain a dozen or more items, four stand out in particular. They are water availability, strategic defensibility, nearby natural resources, and transportation routes.[1]

The previous chapter has made the reader well aware of the critical shortage of water in this region. The availability of suitable water became a primary factor in determining where people would live. Because the transportation of water from one place to another was prohibitive, except when the culture and economy allowed for a major public works project, people typically tended to settle together near a source of fresh water, like a spring or a well. Given the paucity of such water sources, these sites became magnets for urbanization during the biblical period.

Strategic defense also plays a role in the location of a city. The geography of Israel limits the number of entry points into the country, so key cities are located in places where they can function as gateways controlling access to the land. That is certainly an important factor in the founding of cities like Dan, Beersheba, Arad, Jericho, and Beth Shan. They provided border control for the country. But more often, the location of a city was influenced by the natural defenses that offered protection from invaders who had gotten past those border cities. For example, rising terrain was favored as a building location because it required less wall construction to achieve the same level of defensive security. Given the resources available to the ancient soldiers, gravity becomes a key player. You would always want the opposing soldiers to fight their way uphill while you fired upon them from above. This diminished the effective distances of their weapons while increasing the effective distance of your own. The desirability of locating a city on rising terrain clearly influenced the location of cities like Samaria and Masada. Unfortunately, the location of a city on rising terrain also has a downside as it distanced the residents from the springs and wells that were more prominent in the valleys.

The availability of natural resources is a third settlement factor influencing the location of cities and villages. The need to harvest agricultural crops for food makes it desirable to locate cities and villages near fields that will produce valuable food crops. The long history of Bethlehem is closely linked to the wonderful farm fields adjacent to it. (See photo 13.) In such cases, the villages themselves are built on the rocky hillsides that rise above the fields, following the axiom that one dare not build a house where one can grow field crops. The city of Jericho represents another unique study. This city that has existed on the same spot since the eighth millennium BC offers its residents not only an abundant supply of drinking water but also the opportunity to harvest minerals from the Dead Sea region.

The fourth settlement factor that can influence the location of a biblical city is its proximity to a transportation artery. Roadways tend to follow the easiest routes through the country. Urban centers would often develop along such roadways. The residents of these cities would profit either through taxation of the goods being moved on the highway or by providing services that would aid the merchants and travelers moving along that roadway. Undoubtedly, this factor played a major role in establishing cities like Jezreel and Gaza.

TEL FORMATION

Settlement factors like those described above attracted the ancient city builders to a building site. The more of these factors that were present, the more desirable the location was for city formation. This, again, is a place where our local geographical experience likely differs from those who lived in ancient Israel. Where you live, multiple settlement factors may be present in many places, allowing for the establishment of cities in a variety of locations. In Israel, the association of multiple settlement factors is very rare. Where it does happen, cities and villages tend to establish and reestablish themselves. If an invading army comes into the land with the intention of staying, they may destroy a city and its defenses, only to find it necessary to rebuild their new city on exactly the same location. This repeated construction of urban centers on the same location eventually created an artificial hill called a "tel." Such a tel (also "tell") can be anywhere from a few feet high to over 200 feet high depending upon how often a new city was established. For example, the tel at Beth Shan is over 250 feet high and contains at least 20 settlements dating from 5,000 BC. A tel like this becomes a virtual time capsule; evidence of various cultures is sealed and awaits discovery by future archaeologists who carefully dig through the layers hoping to learn more about the history and culture of those who lived in that spot.

TOPONYMY

How is it possible for us to know the name of a tel, or presume to know where to find a biblical city, if there are no posted signs? The study of place names and the linking of those place names to a specific location on the map is called "toponymy." In fact, we do not know the exact location of all the cities mentioned in our Bible. Over twenty years ago, scholar Yohanan Aharoni made the observation that of the 475 place names mentioned in the Old Testament, only about 262 had been positively linked to a specific geographical location.[2] Since then, further progress has been modest due to several difficulties.

First, there are instances where a community has changed location but retained the name. This is clearly the case with Jericho where the Old Testament city and the New Testament city are found in related but separate locations. Second, other communities have remained in the same location but changed their name. For example, Old Testament Shechem becomes New Testament Sychar. Changes like these can even occur within the Old Testament itself. For example, Kiriath Arba becomes Hebron and Laish becomes Dan. Finally, there is the problem of homonymy. In this case, the same name may be used for two or more completely unrelated cities. We may find a number of cities named "Kadesh" in the Bible. As *kadesh* is the Hebrew word for a sanctuary, it may be applied to any number of cities that functioned as a worship center.[3]

Despite these challenges, it is still possible for us to identify the location of over half the named cities and villages in our Bible. A place name in the Bible may be linked with a map in three ways: (1) by noting the survival of the biblical name either on or near the location of the biblical city; (2) by combining literary and geographical clues; and (3) by using archaeological evidence.[4]

In the first case, the name of the biblical city is preserved in the area to the modern time. This may mean that the name of the city itself has persevered, as in the case with Jerusalem or Bethlehem. Or it may mean that a form of the name has been preserved within the area. For example, establishing the location of biblical Beth Shemesh was feasible due to the preservation of this ancient city's name on the modern spring, Ain Shems, which lies adjacent to the biblical site. Identification of the Old Testament city, Gibeon, was possible because of the way its name survived in the modern Arabic city that surrounds the ancient tel. The modern city is named El-Jib. Such preservation of the city's name, either in whole or in part, has led to more positive site identification than by any of the other methods.[5]

When a form of the name has not survived, toponymy must pursue another line of evidence. Literary and geographic clues may be combined to propose a location. Lists of cities can be found in a variety of ancient biblical and secular texts. Of particular value are the lists of cities that mark a territorial border, or lists of cities that describe an ancient travel itinerary. If we are certain about the names and locations of a couple of cities, we may then begin to figure out the names of surrounding cities by following the order suggested in the border or itinerary list.

Finally, archaeology may be used to either initiate or validate a location. There are a few rare instances where the name of the city itself has turned up in the archaeological evidence. Those who were investigating the ancient tel at el-Jib became further convinced that they were on the site of ancient Gibeon when they found the name "Gibeon" engraved on storage jugs within that city. But more often, archaeology is used to confirm the association of a site and name by demonstrating size and occupation dates that are commensurate with other descriptions we have of a city.[6]

HOME CONSTRUCTION

Geography also plays an important role in determining how people constructed their homes. We frequently read about events associated with the homes of biblical characters, but we do not necessarily receive clear descriptions of what those homes were like. An awareness of geography and information gleaned from archaeological investigations allows us to learn something about the places they called home.

From the time of Abraham through the time of Joshua, the people of Israel were primarily Bedouins who moved seasonally with their animals. Their primary shelter was the very portable tent that they had constructed from animal skins. But once the Israelites came to settle in the land, they began to build more permanent structures. When they did, they employed raw materials that were the least expensive and the easiest to acquire: stone, mud, wood, reeds, and branches.

While the patriarchs would have lived in their tents for most of the year, there is one primitive form of architecture that they probably would have used. In the Negev, the foundations of small, round houses dating from the Middle Bronze period have survived to this day. The foundations of these homes are circles up to 5 meters in diameter.[7] In the center of this round foundation is a stone pillar extending about 1 to 1.5 meters in height. Tree limbs would be laid out like bicycle spokes from this center pillar to the round foundation and flat stones would be placed on those limbs to create a roof. The result is a small stone igloo that may have served as a temporary camp for the Bedouin.[8]

The most commonly built private residence during the time of the monarchy in Israel was the Israelite House (also called the Four-Room House or the Pillared House).[9] (See photo 19.) The materials for building such a residence were determined by the region. Stone was used in the mountains, but mud brick was dominant in the valleys.[10] Private residences typically did not have the large shaped stones (ashlars) we associate with the royal building projects. Rather, the stones used for domestic construction were gathered from the surface and employed in whatever shape nature had already given them. Some walls were built entirely of fieldstones. But if mud brick was used in the construction, it rose above such a fieldstone foundation. The bricks themselves were shaped in wooden forms and baked in the afternoon sun. Mud was mixed with sand and straw to improve consistency, to avoid cracks during the drying process,[11] and to prevent the bricks from adhering to the molds.[12] The bricks would be mated to one another by using either a raw mud or lime plaster.[13]

While the raw materials for this type of building were easy to obtain, the maintenance work on a mud brick structure was very time consuming. In order to prevent the brick from degrading through contact with wind and rain, such a structure would be completely plastered over on an annual basis. Ezekiel makes reference to this process when criticizing false prophets. He likens their message to a person who builds a poorly constructed wall and then covers up the poor construction with plaster (Ezekiel 13:10–12). The plaster itself was made by burning limestone in order to make caustic lime. When water is added to this form of lime, the result is slaked lime that can be used as plaster. This process of burning limestone into plaster is mentioned in metaphors of judgment by two of the prophets (Isaiah 33:12 and Amos 2:1).

The typical Israelite home was rectilinear in shape with up to four rooms providing shelter for a family of five to seven people.[14] The surviving foundations indicate that there were four separate rooms on the ground floor of such a home. Lines of stone pillars set off three parallel rooms in the front of the house and one broadroom in the back of the house that was perpendicular to the three front rooms.[15] There is some debate on whether the center room of the three perpendicular rooms was enclosed[16] or was left as an uncovered courtyard.[17] But there is a consensus of opinion that the side rooms on the ground floor were used both for sheltering the family's domestic stock and for general storage. Each family in Israel would have had a small collection of domestic animals like sheep and donkeys. The warmth provided by these animals on a cold winter night was enough of a reason for them to be included within the family residence.[18] A second story provided the living and sleeping quarter of the family.

The roof of the building was also composed of materials that were easily and cheaply obtained. This is where wood was most likely to enter the construction process. Wood beams were laid across the walls of the structure at right angles to one another. This latticework was covered by branches, canes, and palm fronds before a final layer of mortar and clay was added to the top. Such a roof was not merely designed to keep the elements out, but also functioned as additional living and storage space.[19]

Similar materials and techniques were used in building private residences of the New Testament period. However, regional variations again are apparent. For example, in Bethlehem, we have seen how caves were used as the foundations of private homes. (See photo 14.) The Church of the Nativity in Bethlehem is built over such a cave associated with the traditional home of Jesus' birth.[20] An early Christian tradition also points to a cave in Nazareth as the home of Jesus' mother. The Gospel writers report that the angel Gabriel visited Mary at her home in Nazareth to announce to her that she would give birth to the Son of God (Luke 1:26–38). Today, the Church of the Annunciation commemorates that event in Mary's life. It rests over several caves that were used as homes in the first century. Such caves served as the inner room of the house while a wood and stone facade covered with thatch presented as the front of the home.[21]

In communities like Korazin and Capernaum, basalt served as the primary building stone because it was very durable. But when the material is used for roof beams, it becomes very weak. As basalt beams have a tendency to crack when used to bridge a wide room, the rooms spanned by basalt beams are much narrower than other contemporary domestic rooms. This type of architecture was used in cities like Korazin and Capernaum. But like residents in other parts of the country, the citizens of these cities needed a living space larger than those narrow rooms. This problem was solved via the insula design. The insula home consists of narrower rooms that are built around a much larger, open courtyard at the center of the complex. Each room radiating off the courtyard has a single story with a flat, thatched roof. This is clearly the type of home we should have in mind when we read about Jesus healing the paralyzed man in Luke 2:1–12. Apparently, Jesus was teaching in one of the smaller rooms that was able to accommodate only a few people. So many people gathered in the central courtyard outside to hear that those wishing to bring the physically-challenged man to Jesus were unable to get through. This led them to the roof where they tore open the thatch covering and lowered the man into the room.

As the residents of the biblical world began to gather into cities and villages, they did so under the influence of geography. Settlement factors predicted where those cities would be located and predicted the formation of tels, as one community would establish itself upon the ruins of the last. When those residents built their homes, they also were influenced by geography when they selected their building materials from the natural resources around them, and designed their homes in ways that were unique to their geographical setting.

15

TRAVEL AND TRANSPORTATION

As we meet the people of the Bible in our Scripture readings, we often find them traveling from town to town. For example, Samuel traveled on a circuit between Bethel, Gilgal, and Mizpah functioning as a judge for the people of Israel (1 Samuel 7:15–17). Mary and Joseph traveled from their home in Nazareth to Bethlehem when the Roman government required that a census be taken (Luke 2:4). Jesus traveled repeatedly between Galilee and Judea proclaiming the arrival of God's Kingdom, teaching and healing as He went. Each time people traveled, they were using roadways and a medium of transportation that was significantly affected by the geography of this land.

This chapter will explore the geographical dimensions of travel and transportation during the biblical period. Why did people travel? How exactly did they get from one place to another? What risks were involved in such a trip? Where and how were roadways built during the time of the Bible? We will pursue answers to these questions as well as discuss the three roadways that play the greatest role in shaping the culture and history of this land. In the end, this overview of travel and transportation will leave us with a deeper appreciation of what it meant to travel in the biblical world and will illuminate the Bible stories of people like Samuel, Jesus, and Paul as we read about their travels.

WHY DID PEOPLE TRAVEL?

We begin with the realities of life that motivated people to travel. As we read our Bibles, we find people traveled for some of the same reasons that we travel today, while others traveled for reasons that are very foreign to us. For example, family members went to visit one another, like Mary visiting Elizabeth (Luke 1:39–45). Families also made religious pilgrimages to Jerusalem for annual festivals as Jesus' family did (Luke 2:41). Families were on the move because of famines that made migration necessary, like the patriarchs or Naomi's family (Genesis 41:56–57 and Ruth 1:1). We also read about armies marching on strategic military targets with the intent of achieving critical, national goals (2 Samuel 11:1). Merchants would load their pack animals with the products of one region in hopes that they would make a profit by selling them in another region.

Of all the people who traveled, it was the merchants who put on more miles than anyone else. Some of them were involved in moving local commodities just a short distance between regions. Local exchange would have included agricultural products like barley, wheat, olives, olive oil, grapes, wine, peas, and pomegranates, to name a few.[1] However, the geographical position of Israel meant that it was uniquely poised to participate in the world's economy. Thus local merchants also exported agricultural products like grain, oil, and wine to other nations along the International Highway (1 Kings 5:11, Ezekiel 27:17). Still another group of merchants would be passing through the land like the Midianites who drove camels weighed down by spices, balm, and myrrh on their way to Egypt (Genesis 37:25). These same pack animals would then return with a variety of imported products destined for sale among the residents of ancient Israel. These imports included tin, lead, silver, copper, iron, gold, cedar, white linens, gems, ivory, spices, horses, and exotic animals (1 Kings 10:14–19).[2] This type of international travel became an important source of revenue for the government controlling the tax stations along the route. At such stations, a tax based on a percentage of the goods being transported was charged for use of the road. Added protection from bandits and thieves was also provided by military escorts for those who wished to pay an additional fee.[3]

How Did People Travel?

Clearly people traveled for a variety of fundamental reasons, but how did they get from one place to another? The answer to that question is related both to type of terrain expected during the trip and to the wealth of the traveler. Walking was the primary mode of transportation and the least expensive.[4] The distance walked in any given day would certainly be affected by variables like terrain and urgency. But all the evidence supports the fact that people typically walked between 17 and 23 statute miles in a day.[5] This allows us to predict how long a trip would be by measuring the walking distance between two locations and dividing that number by 20.

After travel on foot, the next least expensive means of transportation was the donkey. They were both ridden by individuals and used as pack animals. Although a donkey was considerably less expensive than a horse or camel, their greatest value was to the traveler moving along steep and stony trails.[6] These strong, even-tempered, and sure-footed animals functioned very well on the rocky trails that moved through the interior of the country. But there is also evidence that they were used on longer, overland trips. In such instances, anywhere from 100 to 200 animals were each fitted with 100 pounds of cargo for overland, caravan trips of hundreds of miles on the International Highway.[7]

Camels were also used for transportation because these unique animals were able to handle heavier loads and the extreme conditions encountered during desert travel. (See photo 31.) While a donkey might be able to carry a 100-pound load, a freight camel was capable of carrying between 500 and 600 pounds on its back.[8] These same camels had a very high tolerance for the hot and dry conditions of the desert, allowing them to travel up to 28 miles per day.[9] The camel's ability to tolerate such conditions clearly exceeds that of the donkey due to the unique physical design of this animal that allows for greater tolerance of blowing sand and drought. The wide nostrils of the camel can close to mere slits and the deeply set eyes are guarded by copious lashes. Thus the camel is able to prevent blowing sand from interfering with respiration or vision. Apart from sand, water was a major concern for desert travel. The desiccated, desert conditions can quickly dehydrate both humans and animals while providing precious few opportunities to replenish water supplies. Again the camel has an advantage here as it is able to drink up to 28 gallons of water at one time and travel up to four days without drinking again.[10]

What Risks Did the Ancient Traveler Face?

No matter how one traveled in the ancient world, one thing was for sure: Travel was a difficult and perilous undertaking. Most travel was done during the summer season when the roadways were dry. However, the summer season brings with it intense heat that fatigues travelers and threatens them with dehydration. That is why long-distance travelers and caravans would often avoid the heat of the day by traveling at night.[11] Late spring thunderstorms also affected the trip of the early-season traveler. Although such storms might be occurring miles away, the runoff water caused flash floods that threatened to drown or dash travelers into rocks.

Biblical travelers also faced the risk of personal attack by thieves and wild animals. Jesus spoke about a robbery in His story about the Good Samaritan. Before being aided by a Samaritan man, a Jewish man traveling on the Jerusalem-Jericho road was robbed, stripped, and beaten by thieves (Luke 10:25–37). Wild animals also threatened to prey upon travelers in this land. After Joseph's brothers had sold him as a slave to the Midianite traders, they dipped his robe in the blood of a goat. While this would not have provided a credible alibi for the brothers today, the risk of wild animal attack was so real during Bible times that when Jacob saw the blood on his son's robe, he quickly concluded that he had been killed in this way (Genesis 37:33). As a shepherd who regularly moved his flocks from one pasture to the next, David also encounters lions and bears while tending the family flock (1 Samuel 17:34–35). These and other reported encounters with lions, bears, and wolves make it clear that traveling in the open country of ancient Israel put one at risk of wild animal attack.

It is these travel risks that undoubtedly gave birth to the practice of hospitality that is evident in the biblical culture. Hospitality created a code of reciprocity that obligated the household to provide the needed protection so that when members of that household traveled they would also experience such hospitality from others.[12] Typically the traveler would refuse the first invitation of the host as a sign that the traveler was not a risk to the host. Once the invitation was accepted, the amount of time the traveler could stay was set. This typically was no more than three days.[13] We can see elements of this practice in various biblical narratives and particularly in the hospitality offered in Psalm 23.

How Were Ancient Roadways Built?

Routes

Whether traveling on foot, donkey, or camel, the travelers of the biblical world tended to follow the same routes year after year. The broken landscape of the Promised Land makes it difficult to forge new routes or modify old ones in any meaningful way.[14] Thus just as the location of cities was determined by several key settlement factors, so the establishment of roadways was strongly impacted by geographical realities as well.

Traditionally roads form between places that people spend most of their time. Therefore it is not surprising to find that most ancient roadways connect neighboring cities and villages. A direct route between such places was always the most desirable route. Because Israel is a land with great diversity in elevation, most roadways were established in places that kept the number of tiring climbs and descents en route to a minimum. Thus travelers preferred to follow valleys, particularly chalk valleys, as they offered the driest and softest surface for walking. When the valley floors in a region became too convoluted or rugged to be efficient transportation routes, the travelers would move up to the ridgelines following the watershed of the mountains. Here elevation changes were required, but the changes were not as significant as those demanded by more direct routes that required hopping consecutive ridges.[15] In a few instances, a direct mountain crossing was necessary. In those instances, a mountain pass would be favored by the travelers because it reduced the elevation change required to transition an area. A direct route over the mountain meant not only battling elevation but also thick vegetation. This was certainly the case with the route over the summit of Mount Carmel. For it required both a significant change in elevation as well as fighting through a thick, entangling thicket that ringed the summit of this rising terrain.

Most of the extended traveling would occur in the dry summer months, so water availability would also impact route selection. For example, the shortest route through the Judean Wilderness might not be the most desirable route if water resources were not available on that line of march. Where drainage was inadequate, too much water could also impact the location of a roadway. Muddy trails were not only more difficult to walk, they also were a breeding ground for malaria-carrying mosquitoes.

Consequently, traffic would move up on the edges of the hills and ridge-lines when swamps or muddy plains made travel more threatening or difficult.[16] This was clearly the case with the International Highway as it detoured around the forested swamps of the Sharon Plain.

Some trips required the crossing of a river or seasonal stream. As there were no bridges in the Promised Land until the Roman period, that meant finding a place to cross that either had a ferry or ford.[17] While a river might be crossed at more than one location, certain fords were favored above others due to the shallowness of the water, slower current, and bottom composition that offered more sure footing.[18] Thus the routing of an ancient road that involved a river crossing was substantially influenced by the location of such a ford.

Construction Techniques

As roadways functioned in more than one way, different types of roadways were established and developed to suit different users. Three different road types may be noted: the international roadway, the intra-regional roadway and the local roadway.[19] The international roadways served the more autonomous soldiers and international traders. They looked for an easy and direct route through the country and did not depend on the local populace for support of their trip. By contrast, intra-regional roads and local roads served local families, herdsmen, and traders who handled topographical obstacles more easily but also turned to the local populace for food, water, and shelter during their trip.[20]

Each of these roadways had their own characteristic appearance. But none of them approaches the nature or appearance of a modern, back-country road much less the national freeway system we enjoy. The most advanced roadways of the biblical world were little more than dirt paths that had been cleared of stones and fallen timber.[21] During the Old Testament period, some use of paving stones is evident within cities, but this same paving was not used on any open roads that we know of.[22] That means that even the international roadways were unimproved, dusty beaten paths during the Old Testament period. In the New Testament, the Romans made major improvements in the primary road system within Israel leveling the ground, installing curbing drainage, and paving stones.[23] Even these Roman roads, advanced for their day, would not have impressed the modern traveler.

Of course, the amount of use and type of use would give roadways varying appearances. The international roads of Iron Age Israel were typically wide enough to allow two vehicles to pass, making them 3–4 meters in width. Secondary roads would be only one lane wide, making them about half the size of the international roads. Direct tracks and lanes were less than 1.5 meters in width.[24]

Primary Roadways

Ancient Israel was a tangle of secondary roads and tracks connecting small villages and a web of pathways connecting pastures and agricultural fields. But most of the traffic moving through the country would use one of the three primary roadways we will discuss now: the International Highway, the King's Highway, and the Ridge Road.

The International Highway

The International Highway (also called the Great Trunk Road, the Coastal Highway, and the Way of the Sea or Via Maris) travels via the easiest route through the landscape of ancient Israel. This highway stretches over 1,770 miles from ancient Ur to the southern reaches of Egypt.[25] It travels through Israel because the Promised Land functions as a land bridge between Asia, Africa, and Europe providing a narrow corridor of land between the water of the Mediterranean Sea and the Syrian Desert. Coming from Egypt, ancient travelers would enter the Promised Land near Gaza and use the gently rolling Coastal Plain for the journey north. The swampland and forests of the Sharon Plain forced the roadway eight miles east onto the lower slopes of the central mountains.[26]

As the traveler looked north from here, there loomed the most significant obstacle to a north-south travel through the Promised Land, Mount Carmel. The immense ridge of Mount Carmel cut off easy travel through the plain and demanded that the traveler either climb or circumvent the limestone obstacle. The difficulty of climbing over the top is characterized in the words of William Thomson,

> Ascending from the south, we followed a wild, narrow wadi overhung with trees, bushes and tangled creepers, through which my guide thought we could get to the top. But it became absolutely impracticable, and we were obliged to find our way back again. And even after we reached the summit, it was so rough and broken in some places, and the thorn bushes

too thick and sharp, that our clothes were torn, and our hand and faces were severely lacerated; nor could I see my guide at times ten steps ahead of me.[27]

An alternative route followed the lower flanks of Mount Carmel to the west taking the traveler to Acco and then on to the Ladder of Tyre en route to Phoenicia, but this route was also difficult and less than direct.[28] The best, but in many ways the most dangerous route, was via the Wadi 'Iron that connected Aruna and Megiddo. The elevation gain by means of this pass was more modest and the route was shorter but the path itself was extremely narrow, creating vulnerability for the traveler. When the Egyptian Pharaoh, Thutmose III, used this route, he only did so with great apprehension realizing that his cavalry would have to proceed single file through the narrow defiles of the canyon.[29]

Once past Megiddo, the road took one of two routes. The more frequently used route traveled eastward down the Jezreel Valley toward the cities of Jezreel and Beth Shan. From Beth Shan the traveler could either cross the Jordan River and take the King's Highway to Damascus or continue north up the Jordan River Valley around the northwest side of the Sea of Galilee, turning northeast below Hazor on the way to Damascus. The alternative route that was used less frequently[30] crossed the Jezreel Valley in the direction of Mount Tabor and Mount Moreh, past the Horns of Hattin and below the Arbel Cliffs joining the Jordan Valley just north of Tiberias.[31]

King's Highway

The International Highway was clearly the route of choice for international trade and military movement. But an alternative route did exist that cut a more direct line between the port of Ezion Geber on the Red Sea and Damascus. This highway facilitated movement of perfumes from southern Arabia north across the Fertile Crescent.[32] That route was called the King's Highway (also known as the Sultan's Highway or Trajan's Highway).[33] The primary route of the King's Highway followed the watershed line of the mountains taking advantage of the water and commercial centers along the way. But this route also required the traveler to cross the deep and significant canyons of the rivers that are east of and perpendicular to the Jordan rift valley.[34] An alternative route, sometimes called the Desert Road, lay east of the Jordan rift valley by 25–30 miles. This route avoided the deep canyons. But here on the fringes of the desert, the traveler had to worry about sufficient water resources[35] as well as the threat of raids off the desert.[36] Both routes eventually meet at Amman from which a single road extends to Damascus.

The Ridge Road

The International Highway and the King's Highway were roads primarily used by international traders and armies. But the local people living in the mountains of central Israel also needed a route to travel through their region. That route is called the Ridge Road (also called the Patriarch's Highway because it was widely used by the family of Abraham). This roadway stretches approximately 85 miles from the Negev to the Jezreel Valley following the watershed line of the Judean Highlands. This road begins at the southern gateways to Israel, Beersheba, and Arad. These roads travel north into the hill country and meld as one at Hebron. From Hebron, the Ridge Road literally follows the central ridge of the mountains passing a little more than half a mile west of the Temple Mount in Jerusalem to avoid the deep valleys that surround that city.[37] The road crosses the tribal territory of Benjamin at Gibeon and Bethel before arriving at Shechem. At Shechem the road splits. The western branch arrives at Jezreel via Samaria and Dothan. The eastern branch arrives at Beth Shan via Tirzah and Bezek.[38]

Of the three roadways discussed above, the last is clearly the road used by the greatest number of biblical characters. Abraham walked this road when he entered the land and built altars at Shechem, Bethel, Hebron, and Beersheba as memorials to the promises he was given. He had been promised that his family would become a great nation and own this land. Ultimately, he was promised that from that nation and in that land, the Messiah would be born. For centuries, the family of Abraham would walk the Ridge Road and pass those spots where Abraham personally encountered God. As they passed these altars, they would also be reminded that one day from their own family a unique teacher and prophet would enter the world. This Messiah would be the Savior from sin. How ironic that the same roadway traveled by Abraham and his family would be traveled by Mary and Joseph as they made their way from Nazareth to Bethlehem. That Ridge Road observed the quiet passing of Mary and Joseph making their way to the very place that Micah said Messiah would enter the world

(Micah 5:2). And it is this road, not the International Highway, that Jesus traveled during His earthly ministry visiting with common people between Galilee and Judea and preaching a message that brings us all hope for our eternity. Clearly, Israel was the stage for the greatest rescue mission of all time. That makes this area the land of milk and honey, as well as the land of hope.

NOTES

Chapter 1

1. Barry J. Beitzel, *The Moody Atlas of Bible Lands* (Chicago: Moody Press, 1985), xv.

2. As quoted in Yohanan Aharoni, *The Land of the Bible, A Historical Geography*, 2nd ed., trans. and ed. by A. F. Rainey (Philadelphia: Westminster Press, 1979), x.

3. Aharoni, *Land of the Bible*, ix.

Chapter 2

1. Barry J. Beitzel, *The Moody Atlas of Bible Lands* (Chicago: Moody Press, 1985), 14.

2. Beitzel, *Moody Atlas*, 15. Philip J. King and Lawrence E. Stager, *Life in Biblical Israel* (Louisville, KY: Westminster John Knox Press, 2001), 161. However, see the objection raised by Landesberger. Yohanan Aharoni, *The Land of the Bible, A Historical Geography*, 2nd ed., trans. and ed. by A. F. Rainey (Philadelphia: Westminster Press, 1979), 68.

3. Beitzel, *Moody Atlas*, 14.

4. Aharoni, *Land of the Bible*, 78–79.

5. Beitzel, *Moody Atlas*, 8–13.

6. We understand Numbers 34:10–12 to be a designation of land that has yet to be conquered rather than as an absolute eastern boundary of the Promised Land.

7. Beitzel, *Moody Atlas*, 37.

8. George S. Cansdale, *All the Animals of the Bible Lands* (Grand Rapids: Zondervan, 1970), 36.

9. King and Stager, *Life in Biblical Israel*, 8.

10. K. C. Hanson and Douglas E. Oakman, *Palestine in the Time of Jesus: Social Structures and Social Conflicts* (Minneapolis: Fortress Press, 1998), 104.

11. Efraim Orni and Elisha Efrat, *Geography of Israel*, 3rd ed. (Jerusalem: The Jewish Publication Society of America, 1973), 164.

12. Azaria Alon, *The Natural History of the Land of the Bible* (New York: Paul Hamlyn, 1969), 157.

13. Alon, *Natural History*, 155.

14. Alon, *Natural History*, 115–17.

15. Orni and Efrat, *Geography of Israel*, 164–66.

16. King and Stager, *Life in Biblical Israel*, 94.

17. David M. Cottridge and Richard Porter, *A Photographic Guide to Birds of Israel and the Middle East* (London: New Holland Publishers Ltd, 2000), 4.

18. Cansdale, *All the Animals*, 152.

19. Carl G. Rasmussen, *Zondervan NIV Atlas of the Bible* (Grand Rapids: Zondervan, 1989), 12.

20. Beitzel, *Moody Atlas*, 5.

21. I am thankful to my colleague, Dr. James Martin of Bible World Seminars, for this metaphor.

22. Denis Baly, *The Geography of the Bible: A Study in Historical Geography* (London: Lutterworth Press, 1957), 7.

23. Aharoni, *Land of the Bible*, 10.

24. King and Stager, *Life in Biblical Israel*, 170.

25. Beitzel, *Moody Atlas*, 27.

Chapter 3

1. Richard Cleave, *The Holy Land Satellite Atlas* (Nicosia, Cyprus: Røhr Productions, 1994), 57.

2. Carl G. Rasmussen, *Zondervan NIV Atlas of the Bible* (Grand Rapids: Zondervan, 1989), 60.

3. Barry J. Beitzel, *The Moody Atlas of Bible Lands* (Chicago: Moody Press, 1985), 27. Efraim Orni and Elish Efrat, *Geography of Israel*, 3rd ed.

(Jerusalem: The Jewish Publication Society of America, 1973), 41.

4. Orni and Efrat, *Geography of Israel*, 43.

5. Yohanan Aharoni, *The Land of the Bible, A Historical Geography*, 2nd ed., trans. and ed. by A. F. Rainey (Philadelphia: Westminster Press, 1979), 22.

6. Beitzel, *Moody Atlas*, 27.

7. Denis Baly, *The Geography of the Bible: A Study in Historical Geography* (London: Lutterworth Press, 1957), 129.

8. George A. Smith, *The Historical Geography of the Holy Land* (New York: Harper & Row, 1896), 150.

9. Aharoni, *Land of the Bible*, 24.

10. Orni and Efrat, *Geography of Israel*, 48.

11. Beitzel, *Moody Atlas*, 30.

12. Jerome Murphy-O'Connor, *The Holy Land: An Archaeological Guide: From Earliest Times to 1700*, 4th ed. (Oxford: Oxford University Press, 1998), 161.

13. Baly, *Geography of the Bible*, 139.

14. Jack Pastor, *Land and Economy in Ancient Palestine* (New York: Routledge, 1997), 5.

15. Pastor, *Land and Economy*, 107.

16. Smith, *Historical Geography*, 182.

17. Orni and Efrat, *Geography of Israel*, 37.

18. George A. Turner, *Historical Geography of the Holy Land* (Grand Rapids: Baker Book House, 1973), 152.

19. Smith, *Historical Geography*, 131.

20. Turner, *Historical Geography*, 138.

21. Robert L. Hohlfelder, "Beyond Coincidence? Marcus Agrippa and King Herod's Harbor," *Journal of Near Eastern Studies* 59 (2000): 250.

22. Hohlfelder, "Beyond Coincidence," 249.

23. Hohlfelder, "Beyond Coincidence," 250–251.

24. George S. Cansdale, *All the Animals of the Bible Lands* (Grand Rapids: Zondervan, 1970), 214.

25. Murphy-O'Connor, *The Holy Land*, 236.

26. Aharoni, *Land of the Bible*, 22.

Chapter 4

1. Efraim Orni and Elisha Efrat, *Geography of Israel*, 3rd ed. (Jerusalem: The Jewish Publication Society of America, 1973), 73–74.

2. Carl G. Rasmussen, *Zondervan NIV Atlas of the Bible* (Grand Rapids: Zondervan, 1989), 32.

3. Orni and Efrat, *Geography of Israel*, 73–74.

4. Orni and Efrat, *Geography of Israel*, 78.

5. Orni and Efrat, *Geography of Israel*, 76.

6. Yohanan Aharoni, *The Land of the Bible, A Historical Geography*, 2nd ed., trans. and ed. by A. F. Rainey (Philadelphia: Westminster Press, 1979), 27.

7. Rasmussen, *Zondervan NIV Atlas*, 32.

8. Barry J. Beitzel, *The Moody Atlas of Bible Lands* (Chicago: Moody Press, 1985), 44.

9. Denis Baly, *The Geography of the Bible, A Study in Historical Geography* (London: Lutterworth Press, 1957), 20.

10. Edward Robinson, *Biblical Researches in Palestine and the Adjacent Regions*, 3rd ed. (Jerusalem: Universitas Booksellers, 1970), 3:370.

11. Azaria Alon, *The Natural History of the Bible* (New York: Paul Hamlyn, 1969), 242.

12. Beitzel, *Moody Atlas*, 33.

13. Rasmussen, *Zondervan NIV Atlas*, 32.

14. Beitzel, *Moody Atlas*, 99.

15. Aharoni, *Land of the Bible*, 28.

16. George A. Smith, *The Historical Geography of the Holy Land* (New York: Harper & Row, 1896), 418.

17. Smith, *Historical Geography*, 419.

18. Rasmussen, *Zondervan NIV Atlas*, 33.

19. Beitzel, *Moody Atlas*, 33.

20. Rafael Frankel, *Wine and Oil Production in Antiquity in Israel and Other Mediterranean Countries* (Sheffield: Sheffield Academic Press, 1999), 38.

21. Philip J. King and Lawrence E. Stager, *Life In Biblical Israel* (Louisville, KY: Westminster John Knox Press, 2001), 95.

22. Frankel, *Wine and Oil Production*, 37.

23. King and Stager, *Life In Biblical Israel*, 96.

24. King and Stager, *Life In Biblical Israel*, 97.

25. Frankel, *Wine and Oil Production*, 44.

26. King and Stager, *Life In Biblical Israel*, 71.

27. Jerome Murphy-O'Connor, *The Holy Land: An Archaeological Guide: From Earliest Times to 1700*, 4th ed. (Oxford: Oxford University Press, 1998), 412.

28. The Mishnah is a record of oral teachings by the Rabbis. These teachings explained the meaning and application of the Torah.

Chapter 5

1. Barry J. Beitzel, *The Moody Atlas of Bible Lands* (Chicago: Moody Press, 1985), 35.

2. Richard Cleave, *The Holy Land Satellite Atlas* (Nicosia, Cyprus: Røhr Productions, 1994), 89.

3. Efraim Orni and Elisha Efrat, *Geography of Israel*, 3rd ed. (Jerusalem: The Jewish Publication Society of America, 1973), 53.

4. Orni and Efrat, *Geography of Israel*, 55.

5. Carl G. Rasmussen, *Zondervan NIV Atlas of the Bible* (Grand Rapids: Zondervan, 1989), 36.

6. William M. Thomson, *Central Palestine and Phoenicia*, vol. 2, *The Land and the Book* (London: T. Nelson and Sons, 1883), 238.

7. Thomson, *Central Palestine and Phoenicia*, 37.

8. Yohanan Aharoni, *The Land of the Bible, A Historical Geography*, 2nd ed., trans. and ed. by A. F. Rainey (Philadelphia: Westminster Press, 1979), 29.

9. Rasmussen, *Zondervan NIV Atlas*, 40.

10. Orni and Efrat, *Geography of Israel*, 69.

11. Jerome Murphy-O'Connor, *The Holy Land: An Archaeological Guide: From Earliest Times to 1700*, 4th ed. (Oxford: Oxford University Press, 1998), 357.

12. John A. Beck, "Geography As Irony, the Narrative-Geographical Shaping of Elijah's Duel with the Prophets of Baal," *Scandinavian Journal of the Old Testament*, forthcoming.

Chapter 6

1. Yohanan Aharoni, *The Land of the Bible, A Historical Geography*, 2nd ed., trans. and ed. by A. F. Rainey (Philadelphia: Westminster Press, 1979), 13.

2. Barry J. Beitzel, *The Moody Atlas of Bible Lands* (Chicago: Moody Press, 1985), 34.

3. Efraim Orni and Elisha Efrat, *Geography of Israel*, 3rd ed. (Jerusalem: The Jewish Publication Society of America, 1973), 96.

4. Orni and Efrat, *Geography of Israel*, 146.

5. William M. Thomson, *Central Palestine and Phoenicia*, vol. 2, *The Land and the Book* (London: T. Nelson and Sons, 1883), 242.

6. Carl G. Rasmussen, *Zondervan NIV Atlas of the Bible* (Grand Rapids: Zondervan, 1989), 36.

7. Beitzel, *Moody Atlas*, 34.

8. James B. Pritchard, ed., *The Ancient Near East, An Anthology of Texts and Pictures* (Princeton University Press, 1958), 180.

9. John A. Beck, *Translators As Storytellers: A Study in Septuagint Translation Technique* (New York: Peter Lang, 2000), 181.

10. Jerome Murphy-O'Connor, *The Holy Land, An Archaeological Guide: From Earliest Times to 1700*, 4th ed. (Oxford: Oxford University Press, 1998), 366.

11. Richard Cleave, *The Holy Land Satellite Atlas* (Nicosia, Cyprus: Røhr Productions, 1994), 105.

12. George A. Smith, *The Historical Geography of the Holy Land* (New York: Harper & Row, 1896), 289.

Chapter 7

1. Efraim Orni and Elisha Efrat, *Geography of Israel*, 3rd ed. (Jerusalem: The Jewish Publication Society of America, 1973), 53.

2. Carl G. Rasmussen, *Zondervan NIV Atlas of the Bible* (Grand Rapids: Zondervan, 1989), 42.

3. Barry J. Beitzel, *The Moody Atlas of Bible Lands* (Chicago: Moody Press, 1985), 35.

4. Beitzel, *Moody Atlas*, 44.

5. George A. Smith, *The Historical Geography of the Holy Land* (New York: Harper & Row, 1896), 259.

6. Smith, *Historical Geography*, 425.

7. Richard Cleave, *The Holy Land Satellite Atlas* (Nicosia, Cyprus: Røhr Productions, 1994), 153.

8. Menashe Har-El, *Landscape, Nature, and Man in the Bible* (Jerusalem: Carta, 2003), 77.

9. Philip J. King and Lawrence E. Stager, *Life in Biblical Israel* (Louisville, KY: Westminster John Knox Press, 2001), 100–101.

10. King and Stager, *Life in Biblical Israel*, 113–14.

11. George S. Cansdale, *All the Animals of the Bible Lands* (Grand Rapids: Zondervan, 1970), 46.

12. Victor H. Matthews and Don C. Benjamin, *Social World of Ancient Israel, 1250–587 BCE* (Peabody, MA: Hendrickson, 1993), 57.

13. Rasmussen, *Zondervan NIV Atlas*, 42.

14. William M. Thomson, *Southern Palestine and Jerusalem*, vol. 1, *The Land and the Book* (London: T. Nelson and Sons, 1883), 43.

15. Matthews and Benjamin, *Social World of Ancient Israel*, 55.

16. Jerome Murphy-O'Connor, *The Holy Land, An Archaeological Guide: From Earliest Times to 1700*, 4th ed. (Oxford: Oxford University Press, 1998), 200.

17. The few sentences here will certainly not do justice to the significant history and theology that finds its foundation in this city. A more detailed treatment of the history and archaeology will need to wait its turn in another publication.

18. George A. Turner, *Historical Geography of the Holy Land* (Grand Rapids: Baker Book House, 1973), 18.

19. Menashe Har-El, *Landscape, Nature, and Man in the Bible* (Jerusalem: Carta, 2003), 51.

20. Strabo, *Geography*, 16.2.35–36. Horace Leonard Jones, trans., 8 vols. Loeb Classical Library (Cambridge: Harvard University Press, 1954), 283–84.

21. Rasmussen, *Zondervan NIV Atlas*, 42.

22. Beitzel, *Moody Atlas*, 35.

23. Orni and Efrat, *Geography of Israel*, 66.

24. Rasmussen, *Zondervan NIV Atlas*, 42.

25. Orni and Efrat, *Geography of Israel*, 62.

26. Azaria Alon, *The Natural History of the Bible* (New York: Paul Hamlyn, 1969), 103.

27. Alon, *Natural History*, 99.

28. Yohanan Aharoni, *The Land of the Bible, A Historical Geography*, 2nd ed., trans. and ed. by A. F. Rainey (Philadelphia: Westminster, 1979), 12.

29. Smith, *Historical Geography*, 271.

30. Smith, *Historical Geography*, 263.

31. Aharoni, *Land of the Bible*, 30.

32. Yizhar Hirschfeld, "Spirituality in the Judean Wilderness," *Biblical Archaeology Review* 20 (September—October 1995): 29 and 32.

33. Rasmussen, *Zondervan NIV Atlas*, 43.

34. Murphy-O'Connor, *The Holy Land*, 335.

35. Murphy-O'Connor, *The Holy Land*, 336–37.

Chapter 8

1. Carl G. Rasmussen, *Zondervan NIV Atlas of the Bible* (Grand Rapids: Zondervan, 1989), 47.

2. Rasmussen, *Zondervan NIV Atlas*, 47.

3. Efraim Orni and Elisha Efrat, *Geography of Israel*, 3rd ed. (Jerusalem: The Jewish Publication Society of America, 1973), 65.

4. Jerome Murphy-O'Connor, *The Holy Land, An Oxford Archaeological Guide: From Earliest Times to 1700*, 4th ed. (Oxford: Oxford University Press, 1998), 187.

5. Yohanan Aharoni, *The Land of the Bible, A Historical Geography*, 2nd ed., trans. and ed. by A. F. Rainey (Philadelphia: Westminster Press, 1979), 25.

6. Michael Zohary, *Plants of the Bible* (Cambridge: Cambridge University Press, 1982), 68.

7. Nogah Hareuveni, *Tree and Shrub in Our Biblical Heritage* (Kiryat Ono, Israel: Neot Kedumim Ltd., 1984), 91.

8. Zohary, *Plants of the Bible*, 68.

9. Hareuveni, *Tree and Shrub*, 87.

10. Hareuveni, *Tree and Shrub*, 89.

11. George A. Smith, *The Historical Geography of the Holy Land* (New York: Harper & Row, 1896), 210.

12. Rasmussen, *Zondervan NIV Atlas*, 48.

13. Orni and Efrat, *Geography of Israel*, 65.

14. Barry J. Beitzel, *The Moody Atlas of Bible Lands* (Chicago: Moody Press, 1985), 97.

15. Aharoni, *Land of the Bible*, 26.

16. Orni and Efrat, *Geography of Israel*, 5.

17. Orni and Efrat, *Geography of Israel*, 28.

18. Rasmussen, *Zondervan NIV Atlas*, 49.

19. Orni and Efrat, *Geography of Israel*, 28.

20. Aharoni, *Land of the Bible*, 12.

21. Orni and Efrat, *Geography of Israel*, 28.

22. Rasmussen, *Zondervan NIV Atlas*, 50.

23. Hareuveni, *Tree and Shrub*, 27–33.

24. Hareuveni, *Tree and Shrub*, 24.

25. Rasmussen, *Zondervan NIV Atlas*, 50.

26. Aharoni, *Land of the Bible*, 26.

27. Smith, *Historical Geography*, 280.

Chapter 9

1. Barry J. Beitzel, *The Moody Atlas of Bible Lands* (Chicago: Moody Press, 1985), 37.

2. Beitzel, *Moody Atlas*, 38.

3. Michael Zohary, *Plants of the Bible* (Cambridge: Cambridge University Press, 1982), 105.

4. Nogah Hareuveni, *Tree and Shrub in Our Biblical Heritage* (Kiryat Ono, Israel: Neot Kedumim Ltd., 1984), 93.

5. Azaria Alon, *The Natural History of the Bible* (New York: Paul Hamlyn, 1969), 136.

6. Jerome Murphy-O'Connor, *The Holy Land, An Oxford Archaeological Guide: From Earliest Times to 1700*, 4th ed. (Oxford: Oxford University Press, 1998), 440.

7. Murphy-O'Connor, *The Holy Land*, 174.

8. Carl G. Rasmussen, *Zondervan NIV Atlas of the Bible* (Grand Rapids: Zondervan, 1989), 31.

9. Efraim Orni and Elisha Efrat, *Geography of Israel*, 3rd ed. (Jerusalem: The Jewish Publication Society of America, 1973), 85.

10. George A. Smith, *The Historical Geography of the Holy Land* (New York: Harper & Row, 1966), 481.

11. William M. Thomson, *Central Palestine and Phoenicia*, vol. 2, *The Land and the Book* (London: T. Nelson and Sons, 1883), 450.

12. Alon, *Natural History*, 143.

13. Orni and Efrat, *Geography of Israel*, 88.

14. Beitzel, *Moody Atlas*, 39.

15. Denis Baly, *The Geography of the Bible: A Study in Historical Geography* (London: Lutterworth Press, 1957), 196.

16. Smith, *Historical Geography*, 481.

17. Murphy-O'Connor, *The Holy Land*, 269.

18. The *kinnor* in Hebew is a harp. This name for the lake may be related to the harp-like shape of the lake evident when viewed from the rising terrain that lies above it.

19. Murphy-O'Connor, *The Holy Land*, 429.

20. Orni and Efrat, *Geography of Israel*, 90.

21. Orni and Efrat, *Geography of Israel*, 91.

22. Smith, *Historical Geography*, 462.

23. Rasmussen, *Zondervan NIV Atlas*, 169.

24. Smith, *Historical Geography*, 462.

25. Aharon Kempinksi and Ronny Reich, *The Architecture of Ancient Israel from the Prehistoric to the Persian Periods* (Jerusalem: Israel Exploration Society, 1992), 2.

26. Rasmussen, *Zondervan NIV Atlas*, 35.

27. Mendel Nun, "Ports of Galilee," *Biblical Archaeology Review* 25 (July–August 1999): 19.

28. Strabo, *Geography*, 16.2.45. Horace Leonard Jones, trans., 8 vols. Loeb Classical Library (Cambridge: Harvard University Press, 1954).

29. Mendel Nun, "Cast Your Net Upon the Waters," *Biblical Archaeology Review* 19 (November–December 1993): 51.

30. Nun, "Cast Your Net," 52–53.

31. Nun, "Cast Your Net," 53–55.

32. Jonathan L. Reed, *Archaeology and the Galilean Jesus* (Harrisburg, PA: Trinity Press International, 2000), 184.

33. Beitzel, *Moody Atlas*, 170–71.

34. Murphy-O'Connor, *The Holy Land*, 455.

35. Murphy-O'Connor, *The Holy Land*, 455.

Chapter 10

1. George A. Smith, *The Historical Geography of the Holy Land* (New York: Harper & Row, 1896), 484.

2. Charles F. Pfeiffer and Howard F, Vos, *The Wycliffe Historical Geography of Bible Lands* (Chicago: Moody Press, 1967), 167–68.

3. Smith, *Historical Geography*, 486.

4. Carl G. Rasmussen, *Zondervan NIV Atlas of the Bible* (Grand Rapids: Zondervan, 1989), 54.

5. Rasmussen, *Zondervan NIV Atlas*, 54.

6. Smith, *Historical Geography*, 486.

7. W. F. Lynch, *Narrative of the United States' Expedition to the Jordan River and the Dead Sea* (Philadelphia: Lea and Blanchard, 1849), 264–65.

8. Smith, *Historical Geography*, 486.

9. Efraim Orni and Elisha Efrat, *Geography of Israel*, 3rd ed. (Jerusalem: The Jewish Publication Society of America, 1973), 98.

10. Barry J. Beitzel, *The Moody Atlas of Bible Lands* (Chicago: Moody Press, 1985), 40.

11. Rasmussen, *Zondervan NIV Atlas*, 54.

12. Azaria Alon, *The Natural History of the Bible* (New York: Paul Hamlyn, 1969), 150.

13. Smith, *Historical Geography*, 496.

14. Rasmussen, *Zondervan NIV Atlas*, 52.

15. Rasmussen, *Zondervan NIV Atlas*, 54.

16. Rasmussen, *Zondervan NIV Atlas*, 171.

17. Beitzel, *Moody Atlas*, 170.

18. Jerome Murphy-O'Connor, *The Holy Land: An Oxford Archaeological Guide: From Earliest Times to 1700*, 4th ed. (Oxford: Oxford University Press, 1988), 226.

19. Rasmussen, *Zondervan NIV Atlas*, 44.

20. Lynch, *Narrative of the United States' Expedition*, 275.

21. Orni and Efrat, *Geography of Israel*, 102.

22. Beitzel, *Moody Atlas*, 41.

23. Smith, *Historical Geography*, 501.

24. Murphy-O'Connor, *The Holy Land*, 227.

25. Beitzel, *Moody Atlas*, 41.

26. Murphy-O'Connor, *The Holy Land*, 226.

27. Orni and Efrat, *Geography of Israel*, 45.

28. Rasmussen, *Zondervan NIV Atlas*, 45.

29. Murphy-O'Connor, *The Holy Land*, 229.

30. Beitzel, *Moody Atlas*, 41.

31. Murphy-O'Connor, *The Holy Land*, 288.

32. Michael Zohary, *Plants of the Bible* (Cambridge: Cambridge University Press, 1982), 61.

33. Philip J. King and Lawrence E. Stager, *Life in Biblical Israel* (Louisville, KY: Westminster John Knox Press, 2001), 104.

34. Zohary, *Plants of the Bible*, 60.

35. Beitzel, *Moody Atlas*, 95.

36. Murphy-O'Connor, *The Holy Land*, 386.

37. Murphy-O'Connor, *The Holy Land*, 383.

Chapter 11

1. Carl G. Rasmussen, *Zondervan NIV Atlas of the Bible* (Grand Rapids: Zondervan, 1989), 51.

2. Rasmussen, *Zondervan NIV Atlas*, 51.

3. Efraim Orni and Elisha Efrat, *Geography of Israel*, 3rd ed. (Jerusalem: The Jewish Publication Society of America, 1973), 30.

4. Orni and Efrat, *Geography of Israel*, 151.

5. Orni and Efrat, *Geography of Israel*, 31.

6. Orni and Efrat, *Geography of Israel*, 173.

7. Yohanah Aharoni, *The Land of the Bible, A Historical Geography*, 2nd ed., trans. and ed. by A. F. Rainey (Philadelphia: Westminster Press, 1979), 36.

8. Richard Cleave, *The Holy Land Satellite Atlas* (Nicosia, Cyprus: Røhr Productions, 1994), 187.

9. Rasmussen, *Zondervan NIV Atlas*, 51.

10. Rasmussen, *Zondervan NIV Atlas*, 50–51.

11. Orni and Efrat, *Geography of Israel*, 24.

12. Barry J. Beitzel, *The Moody Atlas of Bible Lands* (Chicago: Moody Press, 1985), 37.

13. John A. Beck, "Geography and the Narrative Shape of Numbers 13," *Bibliotheca Sacra* 157 (2000): 271–80.

14. John A. Beck, "Why Did Moses Strike Out? The Narrative-Geographical Shaping of Moses' Disqualification, Numbers 20:1–13," *Westminster Theological Journal*, forthcoming.

Chapter 12

1. Yohanan Aharoni, *The Land of the Bible, A Historical Geography*, 2nd ed., trans. and ed. A. F. Rainey (Philadelphia: Westminster Press, 1979), 37.

2. Aharoni, *Land of the Bible*, 36.

3. Aharoni, *Land of the Bible*, 38.

4. George A. Smith, *The Historical Geography of the Holy Land* (New York: Harper & Row, 1896), 615.

5. Efraim Orni and Elisha Efrat, *Geography of Israel*, 3rd ed. (Jerusalem: The Jewish Publication Society of America, 1973), 117.

6. Orni and Efrat, *Geography of Israel*, 114.

7. Carl G. Rasmussen, *Zondervan NIV Atlas of the Bible* (Grand Rapids: Zondervan, 1989), 29.

8. Smith, *Historical Geography*, 613.

9. Orni and Efrat, *Geography of Israel*, 114.

10. Orni and Efrat, *Geography of Israel*, 113.

11. Rasmussen, *Zondervan NIV Atlas*, 52.

12. Aharoni, *Land of the Bible*, 38.

13. Smith, *Historical Geography*, 558.

14. Orni and Efrat, *Geography of Israel*, 113.

15. Smith, *Historical Geography*, 522.

16. Rasmussen, *Zondervan NIV Atlas*, 52.

17. Aharoni, *Land of the Bible*, 38.

18. Rasmussen, *Zondervan NIV Atlas*, 55.

19. Smith, *Historical Geography*, 558.

20. Rasmussen, *Zondervan NIV Atlas*, 55.

21. Aharoni, *Land of the Bible*, 40.

22. Rasmussen, *Zondervan NIV Atlas*, 55.

23. Orni and Efrat, *Geography of Israel*, 108.

24. Rasmussen, *Zondervan NIV Atlas*, 56.

25. Orni and Efrat, *Geography of Israel*, 108.

26. Orni and Efrat, *Geography of Israel*, 110.

27. Rasmussen, *Zondervan NIV Atlas*, 56.

28. Aharoni, *Land of the Bible*, 40.

Chapter 13

1. Ewan W. Anderson, *The Middle East, Geography and Geopolitics* (New York: Routledge, 2000), 289.

2. Priit J. Vesilind, "Water, The Middle East's Critical Resource," *National Geographic* (May 1993): 48.

3. Yohanan Aharoni, *The Land of the Bible, A Historical Geography*, 2nd ed., trans. and ed. by A. F. Rainey (Philadelphia: Westminster Press, 1979), 9.

4. Efraim Orni and Elisha Efrat, *The Geography of Israel*, 3rd ed. (Jerusalem: The Jewish Publication Society of America, 1973), 146.

5. Orni and Efrat, *Geography of Israel*, 148.

6. Orni and Efrat, *Geography of Israel*, 148.

7. Aharoni, *Land of the Bible*, 9.

8. In the Wilderness of Zin, springs are more likely to form due to the fact that artesian water pressure has pushed deeper water to the surface. Arie Issar, *Water Shall Flow from the Rock: Hydrogeology and Climate in the Lands of the Bible* (New York: Springer-Verlag, 1990), 113.

9. Philip J. King and Lawrence E. Stager, *Life in Biblical Israel* (Louisville, KY: Westminster John Knox Press, 2001), 124.

10. King and Stager, *Life in Biblical Israel*, 124.

11. King and Stager, *Life in Biblical Israel*, 125.

12. King and Stager, *Life in Biblical Israel*, 127.

13. King and Stager, *Life in Biblical Israel*, 126.

14. Daniel Hillel, *Rivers of Eden* (New York: Oxford University Press, 1994), 66.

15. Carl G. Rasmussen, *Zondervan NIV Atlas of the Bible* (Grand Rapids: Zondervan, 1989), 19.

16. Aharoni, *Land of the Bible*, 240.

17. Jerome Murphy-O'Connor, *The Holy Land, An Oxford Archaeological Guide: From the Earliest Times to 1700*, 4th ed. (Oxford: Oxford University Press, 1998), 386.

18. Issar, *Water Shall Flow*, 179–80.

19. King and Stager, *Life in Biblical Israel*, 213.

20. Issar, *Water Shall Flow*, 173.

21. Murphy-O'Connor, *The Holy Land*, 215–16.

22. Barry J. Beitzel, *The Moody Atlas of Bible Lands* (Chicago: Moody Press, 1985), 46.

23. For an extended treatment of this topic see Leila Leah Bronner, *The Stories of Elijah and Elisha As Polemics Against Baal Worship* (Leiden: E. J. Brill, 1968).

24. Beitzel, *Moody Atlas*, 49.

25. Aharoni, *Land of the Bible*, 8.

26. Orni and Efrat, *Geography of Israel*, 139.

27. Rasmussen, *Zondervan NIV Atlas*, 24.

28. Denis Baly, *The Geography of the Bible: A Study in Historical Geography* (London: Lutterworth Press, 1957), 84.

29. Baly, *Geography of the Bible*, 84.

30. George A. Smith, *The Historical Geography of the Holy Land* (New York: Harper & Row, 1896), 67.

31. Jim Flemming, *The World of the Bible Gardens* (Jerusalem: Biblical Resources, 1999), 13.

32. Orni and Efrat, *Geography of Israel*, 155.

33. Smith, *Historical Geography*, 65.

34. Anderson, *Middle East, Geography and Geopolitics*, 46.

35. Baly, *Geography of the Bible*, 47–48; Orni and Efrat, *Geography of Israel*, 140.

36. Beitzel, *Moody Atlas*, 52.

37. R. B. Y. Scott, "Meterorological Phenomena and Terminology in the Old Testament," *ZAW* 64 (1952): 14.

38. Beitzel, *Moody Atlas*, 52.

39. Scott, "Meterorological Phenomena," 14.

40. King and Stager, *Life in Biblical Israel*, 88.

41. Rasmussen, *Zondervan NIV Atlas*, 25.

42. Orni and Efrat, *Geography of Israel*, 142.

43. Smith, *Historical Geography*, 64.

44. Beitzel, *Moody Atlas*, 52.

45. Orni and Efrat, *Geography of Israel*, 147.

46. Scott, "Meterorological Phenomena," 19.

47. Aharoni, *Land of the Bible*, 14.

48. John A. Beck, "Faith in the Face of Famine: The Narrative-Geographical Function of Famine in Genesis," *The Journal of Biblical Storytelling* 11 (2001): 60.

49. Orni and Efrat, *Geography of Israel*, 141.

50. Orni and Efrat, *Geography of Israel*, 141. Anderson, *The Middle East*, 40.

51. William M. Thomson, *The Land and the Book* (London: T. Nelson and Sons, 1883), 262.

Chapter 14

1. Yohanan Aharoni, *The Land of the Bible, A Historical Geography*, 2nd ed., trans. and ed. by A. F. Rainey (Philadelphia: Westminster Press, 1979), 106-107.

2. Aharoni, *Land of the Bible*, 129.

3. Barry J. Beitzel, *The Moody Atlas of Bible Lands* (Chicago: Moody Press, 1985), 55 and 62.

4. Aharoni, *Land of the Bible*, 124.

5. Aharoni, *Land of the Bible*, 129.

6. Aharoni, *Land of the Bible*, 128.

7. Aharon Kempinski and Ronny Reich, ed. *The Architecture of Ancient Israel from the Prehistoric to the Persian Periods* (Jerusalem: Israel Exploration Society, 1992), 82.

8. Amihai Mazar, *Archaeology of the Land of the Bible 10,000–586 B.C.E.* (New York: Doubleday, 1990), 155.

9. Mazar, *Archaeology of the Land of the Bible*, 485.

10. Philip J. King and Lawrence E. Stager, *Life in Biblical Israel* (Louisville, KY: Westminster John Knox Press, 2001), 28.

11. Kempinski and Reich, *Architecture of Ancient Israel*, 5.

12. King and Stager, *Life in Biblical Israel*, 28.

13. King and Stager, *Life in Biblical Israel*, 28.

14. Mazar, *Archaeology of the Land of the Bible*, 489.

15. King and Stager, *Life in Biblical Israel*, 28.

16. King and Stager, *Life in Biblical Israel*, 30.

17. Mazar, *Archaeology of the Land of the Bible*, 385.

18. King and Stager, *Life in Biblical Israel*, 15–16.

19. Kempinski and Reich, *Architecture of Ancient Israel*, 24.

20. Jack Finegan, *The Archaeology of the New Testament: The Life of Jesus and the Beginning of the Early Church* (Princeton: Princeton University Press, 1992), 30.

21. Finegan, *Archaeology of the New Testament*, 49.

Chapter 15

1. Philip J. King and Lawrence E. Stager, *Life in Biblical Israel* (Louisville, KY: Westminster John Knox Press, 2001), 194.

2. David A. Dorsey, *The Roads and Highways of Ancient Israel* (Baltimore: Johns Hopkins University Press, 1991), 5.

3. Carl G. Rasmussen, *Zondervan NIV Atlas of the Bible* (Grand Rapids: Zondervan, 1989), 27.

4. Rasmussen, *Zondervan NIV Atlas*, 6.

5. Barry J. Beitzel, *The Moody Atlas of Bible Lands* (Chicago: Moody Press, 1985), 65.

6. Dorsey, *Roads and Highways*, 14.

7. Beitzel, *Moody Atlas*, 65.

8. Dorsey, *Roads and Highways*, 13.

9. G. S. Cansdale, *All the Animals of the Bible Lands* (Grand Rapids: Zondervan, 1970), 68.

10. Cansdale, *All the Animals*, 68.

11. Beitzel, *Moody Atlas*, 65.

12. Victor H. Matthews and Don C. Benjamin, *Social World of Ancient Israel 1250–587 B.C.E.* (Peabody, MA: Hendrickson Publishers, 1993), 82.

13. Matthews and Benjamin, *Social World of Ancient Israel*, 85–86.

14. Yohanan Aharoni, *The Land of the Bible, A Historical Geography*, 2nd ed., trans. and ed. by A. F. Rainey (Philadelphia: Westminster Press, 1979), 43.

15. Dorsey, *Roads and Highways*, 41.

16. Rasmussen, *Zondervan NIV Atlas*, 14.

17. Dorsey, *Roads and Highways*, 33.

18. Dorsey, *Roads and Highways*, 39.

19. Aharoni, *Land of the Bible*, 43.

20. Efraim Orni and Elisha Efrat, *Geography of Israel*, 3rd ed. (Jerusalem: The Jerusalem Publication Society of America, 1973), 348.

21. Rasmussen, *Zondervan NIV Atlas*, 14.

22. Dorsey, *Roads and Highways*, 26–27.

23. Dorsey, *Roads and Highways*, 27.

24. Dorsey, *Roads and Highways*, 24.

25. Rasmussen, *Zondervan NIV Atlas*, 14.

26. Aharoni, *Land of the Bible*, 50.

27. William M. Thomson, *Central Palestine and Phoenicia*, vol. 2, *The Land and the Book* (London: T. Nelson and Sons, 1883), 238.

28. Aharoni, *Land of the Bible*, 50.

29. James B. Prichard, ed. "The Battle of Megiddo," in *The Ancient Near East, An Anthology of Texts and Pictures* (London: Oxford University Press, 1958), 176.

30. Beitzel, *Moody Atlas*, 67.

31. Aharoni, *Land of the Bible*, 52–53.

32. Aharoni, *Land of the Bible*, 54.

33. Beitzel, *Moody Atlas*, 69.

34. Aharoni, *Land of the Bible*, 54.

35. Aharoni, *Land of the Bible*, 54.

36. Rasmussen, *Zondervan NIV Atlas*, 28.

37. Dorsey, *Roads and Highways*, 123.

38. Aharoni, *Land of the Bible*, 57.

Resources for Further Study

Aharoni, Yohanan. *The Land of the Bible, A Historical Geography*, 2nd ed. Translated and edited by A. F. Rainey. Philadelphia: Westminster Press, 1979.

Aharoni, Yohanan, Michael Avi-Yonah, Anson F. Rainey, and Ze'ev Safrai. *The Macmillan Bible Atlas*, 3rd ed. New York: Macmillan, 1993.

Baly, Denis. *The Geography of the Bible: A Study in Historical Geography*. London: Lutterworth Press, 1957. Reprint, New York: Harper & Row, 1974.

Beitzel, Barry J. *The Moody Atlas of Bible Lands*. Chicago: Moody Press, 1985.

Cansdale, George S. *All the Animals of the Bible Lands*. Grand Rapids: Zondervan, 1970.

Dorsey, David A. *The Roads and Highways of Ancient Israel*. Baltimore: Johns Hopkins University Press, 1991.

Franki, Harry Thomas. *Atlas of the Bible Lands*. Maplewood, NJ: Hammond Incorporated, 1984.

Freeman-Grenville, G. S. P., Rupert L. Chapman III, and Joan E. Taylor, eds. *The Onomasticon by Eusebius of Caesarea*. Jerusalem: Carta, 2003.

Glueck, Nelson. *The River Jordan*. New York: McGraw-Hill, 1968.

Glueck, Nelson. *Rivers in the Desert: A History of the Negev*. New York: Farrar, Straus and Cudahy, 1959.

Har-El, Menashe. *Understanding the Geography of the Bible, An Introductory Atlas*. Edited and expanded by Paul H. Wright. Jerusalem, Carta, 2005.

Hareuveni, Nogah. *Tree and Shrub in Our Biblical Heritage*. Kiryat Ono, Israel: Neot Kedumim Ltd, 1984.

Issar, Arie. *Water Shall Flow from the Rock: Hydrogeology and Climate in the Lands of the Bible*. New York: Springer-Verlag, 1990.

Lynch, W. F. *Narrative of the United States' Expedition to the Jordan River and the Dead Sea*. Philadelphia: Lea and Blanchard, 1849.

Murphy-O'Connor, Jerome. *The Holy Land: An Oxford Archaeological Guide: From Earliest Times to 1700*, 4th ed. Oxford: Oxford University Press, 1998.

Nebenzahl, Kenneth. *Maps of the Holy Land: Images of Terra Sancta Through Two Millennia*. New York: Abbeville Press, 1986.

Orni, Efraim, and Elisha Efrat, *Geography of Israel*, 3rd ed. Jerusalem: The Jewish Publication Society of America, 1973.

Pfeiffer, Charles F., and Howard F. Vos. *The Wycliffe Historical Geography of Bible Lands*. Chicago: Moody Press, 1967.

Rasmussen, Carl G. *Zondervan NIV Atlas of the Bible*. Grand Rapids: Zondervan, 1989.

Ritter, Carl. *The Comparative Geography of Palestine and the Sinaitic Peninsula*, 4 Vols. New York: Greenwood Press, 1968.

Robinson, Edward. *Biblical Researches in Palestine and the Adjacent Regions*, 3rd. ed. 3 Vols. Jerusalem: Universitas Booksellers, 1970.

Simons J. *The Geographical and Topographical Texts of the Old Testament*. Leiden: E. J. Brill, 1959.

Smith, George A. *The Historical Geography of the Holy Land*. New York: Harper & Row, 1896.

Thomson, William M. *The Land and the Book*. 3 Vols. London: T. Nelson and Sons, 1881.

Turner, George A. *Historical Geography of the Holy Land*. Grand Rapids: Baker Book House, 1973.

Zohary, Michael. *Plants of the Bible*. Cambridge: Cambridge University Press, 1982.

SCRIPTURE INDEX